So You Think You Don't Know One?

SO YOU THINK YOU DON'T KNOW ONE?

ADDICTION AND RECOVERY IN CLERGY AND CONGREGATIONS

Nancy Van Dyke Platt and
Chilton R. Knudsen

MOREHOUSE PUBLISHING

Unless otherwise noted, the Scripture quotations contained herein are from the New Revised Standard Version Bible, copyright © 1989 by the Division of Christian Education of the National Council of Churches of Christ in the U.S.A. Used by permission. All rights reserved.

Morehouse Publishing, 4775 Linglestown Road, Harrisburg, PA 17112

Morehouse Publishing, 445 Fifth Avenue, New York, NY 10016

Morehouse Publishing is an imprint of Church Publishing Incorporated.
www.churchpublishing.org

Cover art courtesy of Thinkstock
Cover design by Christina Moore

Library of Congress Cataloging-in-Publication Data

Platt, Nancy Van Dyke.
  So you think you don't know one? : addiction and recovery in clergy and congregations / Nancy Van Dyke Platt and Chilton R. Knudsen.
     p. cm.
  Includes bibliographical references (p.   ).
  ISBN 978-0-8192-2412-5 (pbk.)—ISBN 978-0-8192-2442-2 (kindle)—ISBN 978-0-8192-2443-9 (e-book) 1. Clergy—Alcohol use. 2. Alcoholism—Religious aspects—Christianity. 3. Codependency—Religious aspects—Christianity. 4. Pastoral psychology. I. Knudsen, Chilton R. II. Title.
  BV4399.P53 2010
  261.8'3229—dc22

                              2010030626

Printed in the United States of America

Dedicated to the memory of Frederick Barton Wolf
Sixth Bishop of Maine

CONTENTS

INTRODUCTION

So You Think You Don't Know One?

THIS BOOK WILL DESCRIBE THE PROGRESSION of addiction and codependency in the ordained minister and in the congregation, and then suggest options for recovery and healing along with a return to a state of balance and health. Both an understanding of change and the theological and spiritual concerns of those affected by addiction are also explored as part of the recovery process. This additional information may benefit those church members who feel spiritually alienated by the problems in their membership and their minister. We use the term "minister" in this book in its broadest sense to include lay leaders as well as clergy.

Over the years we have seen congregations' ministries become seriously impaired as the result of alcoholism and addiction in their clergy or lay leaders, codependency in the congregation, and even over-dependence on endowments. Their ministry is usually in shambles and they become the "problem" congregations that dot a diocese or synod. No one knows how matters deteriorated so markedly, and few know the mechanics and process for recovery. The faithful people of God stumble along for years and years, sometimes for generations. Their codependency did not happen all at once and so their life together seems normal, but they do have a secret—addiction—and it is almost never mentioned. Occasionally a few savvy people will come forward and name the problem, but that truth is rationalized or denied outright by the majority of the members. Yet the word *codependency* describes a systematic and progressive response to addiction to the point at which personal survival is jeopardized and controlled by reactions to the addict's behavior. The end result is complete adaptation to the pathology, a situation that may continue to the point of death for both the addict and the codependent—spiritually, emotionally, and physically.

At first we were inclined to blame the alcoholic/addicted minister. After all, everyone else did. One way or another, sometimes by observation, and sometimes by hands-on involvement, we discovered some of the issues that seem to paralyze the "family" or relational systems of these worshiping communities. We have realized after some years of thoughtful reflection that there is not one simple answer as to "Who is to blame?" and as a matter of fact, the blaming itself is not helpful at all.

Recovery is one day at a time; the congregation and the minister did not become impaired over a single day or year. Their honesty with themselves and each succeeding minister will help them continue what grace has begun. Slowly the healthier members of the congregation will help in an appropriate way those who are still struggling toward wholeness. This "critical mass" of wellness and healing will provide strength and hope to the others who follow their example. Vigilance on the part of the local church members and the governing denominational body, as well as regular self-assessment with trained consultants, helps support those who want to seek the healing which is possible. Information and education of all church members can incorporate recovery principles into the congregational norm for healthy relational behavior and spiritual growth.

Many of the studies and references we have used here focus on alcoholism, and therefore that term will be used extensively here. The use of the terms "substance abuse" and "addiction" are also used in this book, sometimes interchangeably. The authors are aware that terms such as "dependency" and "substance dependencies" are currently in use; this terminology has changed to promote clearer understanding in the field of addiction, although the phenomena of addiction itself does not change. With the onset of the use of marijuana, and the hallucinogenic drugs in the 1960s, and with the subsequent increase in use of pain medications, "substance abuse" became the preferred term. The fact of the matter is that both the younger generation and the older generation use alcohol as an aid to prevent withdrawal symptoms when the "hard drugs" are not available. Because it is legal, alcohol may be easily obtained anywhere to calm the anxiety and erratic behavior of an individual whose addiction to preferred other substances has reached the point at which those substances must be used frequently. Addiction to internet pornography, sex, prescription drugs and gambling appear to have a withdrawal pattern similar to alcohol, as evidenced by the addict's anxiety, fragmented behavior, irritability and impaired judgment.

Please be aware that the examples of alcohol, and other addictions used in this book are just that—examples. There are other reasons and other options for the various stages of addictive behavior and recovery. We also wish to note that the case studies are composite stories and the names are fictitious. However the addiction related events are factual.

When we first began our work, moreover, research on the alcoholic minister focused on male clergy. The increasing number of women clergy in mainline denominations has brought a corresponding rise in the incidence of alcoholism/addiction in female ministers, with some variations in substance abuse, but there are fewer studies available. More study needs to be done.

Our gratitude goes to the many authors who have documented the symptoms of addiction and codependency in both individuals and family systems, to friends who have shared their information and stories, and to congregations who have allowed us to see the toll that addiction has taken on their common life and those who have boldly claimed the resurrection of recovery in their lives.

We also wish to acknowledge the help, encouragement, and support of Elizabeth Platt, Regina Knox, and Cynthia Shattuck in the preparation of this manuscript.

CHAPTER ONE

HOW IT ALL BEGINS

The Seeds of Codependency

ONE OF THE BEST IMAGES we have come across to describe the codependent congregation is a collection of people in a large life raft with an addicted person. As the addict alternately rushes from the center to the sides of the raft and back, throws tantrums, or sits in silence, the other people in the life raft struggle to keep their balance by shifting their positions as necessary for survival. These passengers constantly must compensate for the unpredictable movements of the addict. Sometimes they even shift their positions to keep the raft stable by counteracting the movements of the other passengers.

Another commonly used image for the codependent system is that of a mobile, which is perfectly balanced when at rest. When the addict tips the balance point, however, the other figures on the mobile shift and change as well, seeking equilibrium. There is no opportunity for rest and stillness; the addiction seems to take on a life of its own that influences everything the mobile does in order to regain its balance and original state sometimes causing it to swing so wildly that figures drop off the mobile.

The people in the life raft and the figures on the mobile attempt to return their system to a balanced state; in the words of the late Murray Bowen, family therapist and systems guru, they attempt to achieve "homeostasis." There is little sense of the need for order or

1

purpose as most of these behaviors are unconscious efforts to keep the system stable for their own survival. Once in a while someone attempts to help or intervene, but things quickly return to survival mode; such efforts rarely succeed. The "system," whether of a family or a congregation, must find and regain its own balance. To some degree, knowledge, education, and support will help, but the change must occur within the system itself. Denial by the systems members of the key concerns that prevent the congregation's return to normal and healthy life must change to acknowledgement of the problems.

It is important to remember that these behaviors are reactions by powerless individuals to a frightening and confusing series of events in their community life. For a long time they will do whatever they can to make the addict's behavior seem reasonable, believing that they can control what is happening, and that will power is all that is needed.

Certainly the congregational leadership, whether ordained or lay, is only one part of a cluster of codependency, and in no way to "blame" for the fear and anxiety that overtake the congregation's life. In one sense, their emotions mirror the underlying fears and pain that the leader attempts to medicate by his addiction. Their behaviors and feelings are the result of attempts to maintain normalcy without being truly aware of what is normal for the people of God. In addition, these congregations genuinely mean to carry out Jesus' work and follow him, but given that much of their efforts are marred by codependency they fail to grasp the whole message of the gospel and discipleship as a lifestyle. While these words may seem harsh, emotional toll, exhaustion and the spiritual depletion of the individuals in the congregation reveal the pain, fear, and struggle of the codependent congregation.

CASE STUDY: GREG

"Greg does everything." Greg had made himself indispensable in the life of his parish. He arrived at church before anyone else each Sunday morning and got to work turning up the heat, folding the service bulletins, starting the coffee, and checking on the bathrooms.

He showed up at church most Saturdays, too, as the small congregation could not afford a sexton or custodian. Greg was the only volunteer for the weekly dusting, vacuuming, cleaning, and mopping. There used to be two teams of church cleaning volunteers. It was good fellowship: they alternated weeks and went out for lunch together after cleaning the church. Gradually, however, they drifted away as they realized that Greg was willing to do it all and had become so obsessive about cleaning that they got tired of hearing his criticisms.

Most members of the church referred to Greg as "the do-everything guy," a pillar of the church. Greg enjoyed the attention, and actively spoke up at church gatherings about all the things he was getting done around the church. A few people resented his domineering attitude and it bothered them that he chased away people who wanted to volunteer, but they had learned to silence their feelings under pressure from others: What would we do without Greg? The church would crumble if he left! Don't ruffle his feathers!

On rare occasions, someone else would get to church unusually early on Sunday morning. Once it was the organist, who had houseguests that week and hadn't had time to practice the hymns. Another time, a church school teacher came to set up a complicated activity. From time to time, an altar guild worker would come in with a load of freshly ironed altar linens. Each of these early arrivals was greeted briefly and begrudgingly by Greg—"Nothing personal; it's just hard to work with people underfoot."

As time passed, word got around that Greg often smelled of alcohol, especially first thing in the morning, and his hands trembled. Once when an altar guild member searched for a pair of shears to trim some unruly altar flowers, she came across a half-empty bottle of vodka hidden amongst the rags in Greg's custodial closet. Summoning up her courage she asked him about it. "Those kids!" he told her. "They throw all kinds of things into the churchyard on Saturday nights. I was saving them to put into the trash after the service today." She remained uneasy, but she didn't want to get him upset and it wasn't as though he was falling into the gutter. He was an upstanding family man with a good job and a hard worker for the church.

Eventually Greg's alcoholism became the secret everyone knew. He had so thoroughly cultivated the church's dependence that no one dared to confront him. Finally he died of a ruptured esophageal blood vessel and was found on the floor of the church kitchen early on a Sunday morning.

This was a wake-up call for the congregation. As people remembered Greg in the weeks following the funeral, they began to acknowledge the reality of his addiction and their own collusion in the silence surrounding it. They offered good support to Greg's widow and children and the congregation began to heal while they questioned what they could have done for Greg. In what ways did they encourage and enable the disease, what action could they have taken, and what kept them from acting?

The congregation's clergy and lay leaders also went through some brave self-examination about the congregation's culture of secrecy. The old-timers had much to say as frank conversations began about the congregation's past, and they owned up to earlier instances of alcoholic or addicted clergy and lay members. In time the congregation became respected and well known for its ministry with alcoholics, addicts and their families. A number of Twelve Step groups were invited to use the church for their meetings, while educational events about addiction and recovery were offered to the whole community. The next time a church member showed signs of addiction, concerned people sought expert consultation, took responsibility, spoke the truth in love and gave thanks one day at a time for sobriety, for healing, and for new beginnings.

THE SEEDS OF CODEPENDENCY

Generally accepted figures suggest that one alcoholic or addict affects at least four other people around him. Those four become codependent to some degree, depending on the intensity of the bond between them. Codependency means that the lives of these affected have begun to revolve around the addict's behavior. Essentially, they are "addicted" to the addict, who becomes the identified patient or problem. It is inevitable, considering that alcoholism and drug abuse affect more that ten percent of Americans, that these affected and codependent people will find each other whether or not they overtly recognize their common bond. They find each other in our culture and in congregations because they have common norms and understandings of relationships, however healthy or impaired. Some unconscious choices as to joining a particular denomination or church may in fact be the result of an individual's repeated encounter with addiction, which is a provocative thought.

Congregations function in many ways like families, the difference being that congregational membership is voluntary and so individuals have a choice about their membership. Like a family, church members share a common meal, are concerned about others in crisis and remember them in prayer if they are absent, look up to a parental authority figure, and often call themselves "children" of God. They have norms for relational balance—some behaviors or perceptions are simply deemed not acceptable and will separate them from God, from the family system, and from congregational life. Without these norms and boundaries, the life of the congregation then becomes more vulnerable to dysfunction. The more dysfunctional behavior occurs, and the more it is accepted or tolerated, the more the dysfunction insidiously changes the behavior of a family or congregational system.

The key issues in the diagnosis of addiction as well as those of codependency center around the progression of the disease. Progression is marked by frequency and tolerance. Tolerance in the addict is a silent marker of the body's adaptation to the drug of choice, which demands increasing substance or alcohol use to maintain the biochemical imbalance created by their use, thereby avoiding the pain of withdrawal. Most of us recognize sobriety when a person does not drink or use, or intoxication when she is seriously and chronically impaired by addiction. But we are unlikely to see that a person is *progressing* in her addiction unless we have known her for some time. That is true in both the addiction process and the recovery. It is even more difficult to discern the hallmarks of the dysfunction or the relative health of a congregation as it progresses or recovers. We might speculate that tolerance in the codependent is just that—an increasing ability to accept more and more aberrant or unreliable behavior.

Initially, the progression of dysfunction in the addict and in codependent family systems of all kinds seems minimal. Changes are accommodated within the system because they appear to be within the normal range of accepted interaction. There is little concern as long as the function or homeostasis of the family system is perceived by its members to be stable and normal; changes are tolerated. However, a life crisis may very well impact the balance of the family system; the status quo of the system, healthy or diseased, becomes strained and fertile soil for increased dysfunction. The crisis may be the loss of a member, who is now unable to play his part in maintaining the system's balance.

Congregational systems are similar. Codependent congregations begin, as we have said, with unstated norms for its members and the way they relate to one another. Because of the very closeness and strength of family ties in a community, a group of codependent families may establish smaller churches, with a few members of a denomination in the community meeting for worship in their homes and then forming a church. Others in the community join them; family support is important and necessary to founding the fledgling church. Since we may assume that one or more members of that founding group have been affected by addiction, it is most likely that they will bring into their system symptoms of codependency.

GENERATION TO GENERATION

These founding families establish norms for the congregation. They also may have life crises or an encounter with addiction that affects their health and well-being and the unconscious established norms. As generations come and go, family members choose addicted spouses, and the codependent behaviors find rich soil for growth. The dysfunctional behaviors become the norm, not just for the family, but also for the church. Other local families are attracted to the church as a result of compatible behavior in their friends. Social events such as fund-raisers are known for their "party" atmosphere that draws members and their friends from the entire area; the church develops a reputation for good food and good times. A whole generation may be involved in this social life of the congregation. These social members will leave when the congregation begins to heal, returning occasionally or talking with friends as they feel some attachment to the people they knew during that time period, but there will never be any lasting commitment.

Sometimes their clergy or lay leaders evidence early symptoms of addiction, which might include obligatory wine or sherry in regular pastoral visits, frequent verbal references to alcohol, or, in later progression, depression and serious medical or legal problems. When this occurs, the congregational expectations and norms are called into question, and founding family members gradually take control of the parish. They assume more and more of the impaired clergy's tasks, and finally, if necessary, initiate firing of the clergy.

The congregation itself compulsively helps others, often to everyone's detriment. Excellent mission outreach may be extended to many organizations, with fundraisers and worthy causes, but just as personal and spiritual self care are put aside to care for others, so is maintenance of the building deferred. The leadership becomes increasingly weary and the church seeks new members to "share the load."

The adult children of the congregation may return to the church, bringing with them more and more impaired behaviors. Others do not come back, avoiding the friendships of younger days; they are either the less resilient or the healthier progeny. We have seen an entire generation of codependent children who, having lost their minister as the result of his suicide, never returned to the church again. His death was never explained to the youth group, nor were they encouraged to mourn him. Among those who do return, the family "heroes"—children whose good or better behavior was applauded by their families—frequently move into leadership positions and increasingly take over the tasks of their impaired minister while attempting to maintain the life of the congregation. Some smaller congregations may have as many as five generations in church on a single Sunday; one or more of these family members may be hiding an addiction. Others will murmur about their personal or congregational problems, but only occasionally will family loyalty allow truth-telling.

Codependency continues its progression, with blame for conflict or problems placed on those who are impaired by addiction, or lacking that, the convenient scapegoat who can be found in every congregation. Scapegoats will have some outstanding characteristic that deviates from the group norm, may be thought of as eccentric, and will readily accept their role which parallels the role they played in their addicted family system. The congregation as a whole begins to isolate itself from other churches in the area and from the denomination. They deny that there are problems, although some members leave with a variety of excuses that may reach church authorities second or third hand. Gradually the congregation becomes divided between those who took different sides on a particular issue—the music, the youth group, use of church buildings by outside groups, the personality of the church secretary—which may have had little to do with the real issue. This dual personality arises because enough group norms are violated so often that a rival set of norms emerges. A hallmark of the problem will be an approximate fifty/fifty division on the many decisions that are inherent in church life.

Individual needs for power and control, distraction from the real mission of the congregation, and boundary blurring become more and more frequent until dysfunction itself becomes normative. System balance is tentatively achieved around new group norms that include isolation, denial, and low self-esteem. Most importantly, the congregation that has now misinterpreted the message of the gospel: "You shall love the Lord your God with all your heart, and with all your soul, and with all your strength, and with all your mind; and your neighbour as yourself" (Luke 10:27). For although the congregation indeed "loves" their neighbor, they do not love themselves. They have slowly come to idolize and idealize their church, their outreach, their music program, or even the giver of their endowment. But they have not recognized that they are not God, nor is their church. Their love of neighbor, especially those who are poorer or less fortunate than themselves, gives them the false self-esteem that they had lost over the years. They are the caretakers rather than the caregivers. However, they do this caretakeing ministry to their own detriment, often refusing to share their roles with anyone else and they fail to care for themselves or their families appropriately

Other codependent congregations, small or large, have had an addicted minister or lay leader from the beginning, so they seek and attract similar individuals throughout their history. Sometimes they call a codependent minister—after all, he is like them. But any minister that does not fit into the system patterns of reactivity and control will soon be gone. The minister will eventually leave, and the congregation will acknowledge that "they were a poor fit."

CASE STUDY: ST. AIDAN'S

St. Aidan's has a history of addicted and codependent clergy and codependent clergy who leave after a few years with no explanation. One of those has just found a better position outside the state. Before he left he got a divorce which surprised some in the congregation. His wife also had been a minister. Some who had seen him publically chastise her during a worship service were not surprised. The governing body had a formal search process proposed by a consultant through which ministers were called by a congregation. It soon became obvious that the congregation had its own ideas about how the process would be done. Too many members were appointed to the search committee, the chair of the committee asked the consultant to bend the rules with a promise of future advancement, and when the budget was examined to see if the congregation could afford a new priest, the committee "fibbed about their financial status just a little." After all. they told themselves, the new priest would quickly attract new money and that would make up the difference.

They began to interview the clergy names they were given and called a new minister. After a while a story began to circulate about the interviewing process. It was done over cocktails at a private country club—the interviewee was the only one not drinking—and they tried to hire him. Warned by their history, he turned them down. They then called their second choice, who was interviewed in the same way and accepted. A year later, however, when the minister did not receive the salary he had been promised, he openly told the congregation that he was looking for another position and would leave when he found one.

The clergy St. Aidan's hired were also increasingly impaired: each is not only addicted but took on some of the other symptoms embodied in the congregation's norms. These ministers are entertainers, have low self-esteem, are conflict avoidant or communicate poorly. As they grow increasingly proficient at hiding their impairment, the congregation gives itself high scores for doing the clergy's work in leadership, outreach, and community-wide involvement.

As in a marriage or family setting, the minister and the congregation relate to one another on similar levels of impairment. When the addiction of the minister progresses and his spiritual, physical, and mental life deteriorate, so does that of the codependent congregation. Conversely, as the health of the clergy improves, so does the recovery of the congregation.

Another potential root of codependency is the church's endowment, which is usually a large one. Like large memorial gifts, it always has an impact on the congregation's life and sometimes even on their worship space. The gift is analogous to the changes caused in a family that wins the lottery, although sometimes the congregation does not know the benefactor. The power implicit in money and in its control by an individual or foundation cannot be underestimated. The endowment can be used for the "general" fund or for a specific request, but the church governing body is often not consulted in its designation. Endowments express the final wishes of the giver, may be tainted with personal bias, and can significantly alter congregational identity forever. Moreover, the specific bequest may not be at all in accordance with the mission of the congregation or its vision. For example, an oversized organ is given to a church that is far too small for the large instrument. As a result long-standing furniture arrangements must be moved, memorial windows replaced, and the movement of worship altered by the constraints of the pipes, the instrument, and its acoustics. It becomes a source of tension, particularly if the donor is unknown and did not even attend that congregation, but simply liked organ music.

"General fund" endowments can also create dependency in a congregation because the members can avoid the challenge of personal stewardship, relying on the endowment income. Decision-making becomes a power struggle. Sometimes lay people with financial backgrounds form committees to run the endowment for the congregation; they then control how the endowment is used, augmenting the passivity and dependent behavior. Moreover, now that they "have money," the self-image of the congregation's members is inflated, and unrealistic and out of touch. Always in the progression of codependency, relational behavior in the church community becomes less honest, less in touch with reality, and more idolatrous.

As we said above, the congregation tends to develop a "Jekyll and Hyde" personality and no one is ever sure which side will emerge; one will be good and kind, the other evil and vicious. While congregational responses are not as sharply defined as the name implies, there is a fifty-fifty division in their responses. Whether asked to choose a new carpet, or make a choice in getting rid of the minister, half will respond one way and half the other. They will be about equally divided on the profile of persons they would accept for a new minister. The division is the only thing that is predictable; the issues that concern them are not really relevant. Stalemated decision-making assures that change will not happen. On the whole, the congregation is simply responding to change and fears of further imbalance in their family system.

Later on, if the congregation begins to heal, some members of the congregation may form a resistant group that persists from one minister to the next. Although filled with good intentions, it may also include a critical, gossiping contingent that focuses on the new minister or indeed other aspects of the congregation that come into focus for criticism. Interestingly enough, the alcoholic also has a similar "Jekyll and Hyde" personality: when sober, she displays a kind and generous personality, but when drunk, she becomes either combative and hostile or depressed and withdrawn. Intoxication produces a personality that will do things never dreamed of by someone in recovery. That personality may emerge as addiction progresses; the deterioration of the ego function of the minister may lead to acts of adultery, embezzlement, boundary violation, and other unacceptable behavior.

A further source of a congregation's codependency is the sense of adoration created by the leadership of a powerful, charismatic, and engaging minister. Ted Haggard, former pastor of the evangelical New Life Church in Colorado, described its dynamics on national television in 2009. In cases like these a church's success depends on the minister's charm, public image, sense of righteousness, supposed omniscience, and having all the answers. These charismatic ministers build churches, television empires, and healing ministries, establishing a social norm that exists for as long as they continue to attract members and provide a safe haven for their congregation. That congregation is expected to wrap their lives around its "special" mission. Mega-churches may have some of the same dynamics, but their small-group format tends to minimize the "star quality" power of a charismatic leader.

Unlike most evangelical clergy, these fragile "stars" depend on maintaining that success along with their congregations' dependency on them. If and when such a minister falls from grace, the shield of publicity crumbles; it can no longer isolate him from those followers he has dominated through his mystique. The minister's need for dominance and the adoration of his followers may also result in abusive responses to anyone who question the leader's norms for his followers.

One former church administrator, Margie Cash, gives an example of the difficulties of "truth-telling" in such a setting. "When I was working in the church," she writes,

> I was in a position of managerial accountability and responsibility. In many respects, I greatly enjoyed the work; but in many other respects, I found the execution of simple tasks enormously exhausting and depleting. At those times, I tended to confront and rock the boat in ways that were not appreciated by the powers of the church. If someone was being irresponsible about their job, I'd indulge them only so long; then I'd get them into a face-to-face confrontation that attracted a lot of negative attention. Whether I was right or not was usually irrelevant in the eyes of the senior staff; the fact was, I was not "going along." Normal assertiveness was considered subversive; appropriate peer pressure was viewed as an attempt to "take over the church"; and complaints of any kind were sternly dismissed as insubordination.[1]

Cash became the "black sheep" at staff meetings, and was overlooked and shunned by others who needed to curry the minister's favor to maintain their positions. The system conspires to protect its "idol" so that any question of the idol's behavior results in banishment.

---

1. Margie Cash, "Codependency in the Church" (*http://margiecash.com/publications/ codependency-in-the-church-the-dysfunctional-family-of-god/*).

In codependent congregations, the addicted minister is probably the most common underlying factor, but this should never be tagged as the sole cause of congregational dysfunction. The congregation is already fertile soil for one reason or another. They have no resiliency or spiritual foundation, as well as little experience with addiction that would help them to identify the dysfunction caused by their own behavior and that of the minister. Certainly in the early years of progression, especially given the transience of members, evolution of the group norms and the problematic behavior of codependency are subtle. It is often only later, in hindsight, that members recognize what has been happening and may be willing to accept the truth of their dilemma.

> O God, overflowing with mercy and compassion, you lead back to yourself all those who go astray. Preserve your people in your loving care, that we may reject whatever is contrary to you, and may follow all things that sustain our life.
>
> —From the Lutheran Book of Worship,
> Prayer for Lectionary 24, Year C

CHAPTER 2

THE PROGRESSION OF CODEPENDENCY

CASE STUDY: CAROLYN

Carolyn was a newcomer to the church who quickly became known as a "spiritual person.") She often shed tears ("of joy in the Lord," she said) during Sunday worship and her conversation was filled with references to the Holy Spirit. She organized a prayer chain, started a parish healing ministry, and as member of the worship committee helped to write the weekly intercessions offered during worship. Her somewhat histrionic behavior and her continual references to the Holy Spirit, however, eventually drove people away from these ministries.

Over time, people also noticed that Carolyn had one prayer concern that always made its way into the weekly intercessions: "We pray for young people who have lost their way. . . ."

This was the point when Carolyn would weep during the service. The culture of this congregation was kindly, but reserved. They didn't confide in one another about their troubles and burdens, and tended to shrink from emotional excess so she violated a norm. As Carolyn's spirituality became more intrusive, she was harder and harder to be around. But Jean, who some people felt to be too nosey, did not withdraw. One day she took Carolyn out for coffee.

14

"Carolyn," Jean said gently, "I've noticed that you always put in prayers for young people who have lost their way. Is there anyone in particular you are thinking of?" At first hesitant, Carolyn eventually told the painful story of an addicted son who was unable to "get right with the Lord." She spoke of praying constantly for her son, getting prayer chains all over the country to pray for him, undertaking acts of spiritual discipline (fasting, tithing, lighting candles) for his healing. As time passed, and her son continued to drink and use drugs, she ramped up her prayer disciplines and became increasingly histrionic. Her son refused when Carolyn demanded he attend healing services, and the angry exchanges between them escalated.

Jean was the right person to hear Carolyn's story. Slowly, over the next few months, Jean helped Carolyn learn about the disease of addiction and the resulting codependency in people close to an active addict. Carolyn came to understand that shame and guilt about her son had in fact harmed her spiritually and isolated her from others. As her increasing desperation drove her to seek more and more remedies, her spiritual life became increasingly crippled: gratitude, peace, joy, courage, trust, and hope were all crowded out. Carolyn began to attend Al Anon and Nar Anon meetings, finding spiritual balance and learning to detach from her son's disease as she focused on her own recovery. As Carolyn grew healthier, she was able to let go of trying to control her addicted son. And she came to realize how in "my obsession about spiritual practices, I was trying to control God, too." Today the entire congregation benefits from Carolyn's spiritual leadership and her honesty, compassion, trust, and joy.

CODEPENDENCY AND GROWTH

In spite of members who say "We want to grow," increasing the size and vitality of the codependent congregation is difficult. The idea of growth is a source of fear and anxiety for long-time members— what if the new people aren't aware of "how we do things"? The norms and culture of the church are threatened. Newcomers may hold religious views that differ from what others believe, and may even seek already occupied leadership roles. But since Christian norms require that the congregation be "loving," the older members become addicted to appearing and sounding like nice people, so they gossip among themselves about new members and discuss them in covert ways. Such tactical maneuvers, albeit unconscious, are very successful in resisting growth.

One congregation was impaired by a succession of at least five addicted clergy. As a result, whenever any change was suggested, members of the congregation responded with negative and often abrasive remarks: "Why are you doing it this way? It will never work!" "We tried that before, don't you remember?" "Well, if we have to eliminate wine from our monthly gourmet suppers, we just won't have them." Leaders in the congregation were occasionally suspected of having an alcohol problem (they had accidents and attempted to control much of the ministry with erratic, blustering behavior). Their few financial records were poorly kept and had been that way for years; fiscal irregularities and clergy misbehavior was never discussed. However, the congregation never took any responsibility for these problems. One got the impression that their blaming and lack of responsibility was the norm, and for them at that point in their progression, it was true.

In a small congregation, the "gatekeepers"—long-time elderly members who have leadership positions as patriarchs or matriarchs—take it upon themselves to inform new members of the norms. This behavior may in turn discourage the visitor from returning to church altogether by sending a message, in some way, that she doesn't belong here. Even playing "Who do you know?" or "What do you do?" can be done in such a way that the newcomer gets the message that she is not up to their standards. Moreover, these same members know the rules. They are quick to tell newcomers, "We don't do it that way," but rarely tell them how it is done, if they even know; they displace their anxiety onto the newcomer.

The desire for congregational growth also puts more stress on the minister, who may be unable to incorporate new members appropriately and ultimately reveals his own resistance to growth. By placing new members on someone else's "turf," or allowing them to unwittingly offend other members of the congregation by encouraging innovations in worship and polity, the minister sabotages the congregation's growth. The newcomers are attempting to belong, but they bring with them the presuppositions and expectations of their former congregations. They try to implement these in their new congregation in order to relieve their own fear and anxiety over the move into the new community, but usually fail to accomplish that goal. Resistance to change is too entrenched.

The loss of valued long-time members or a founding family creates similar stresses. Long-time members will be likely to have their funeral service at the church. They leave behind a legacy of service, money, and, usually, jobs well done. They leave a place in the pews that will be occupied by their ghosts for several generations; no one else will take the departed members seats. They leave behind their biases—"No fans in the church ceiling"—"no female clergy" that will invoke their memory whenever change or a new way of doing things is mentioned in a congregational meeting. They leave a space in the tasks that they did, and that space is recognized whenever someone else does it differently. Their recipes ("Janice's salad, Nancy's punch") will be used for years at social events and may be immortalized in a cookbook. In addition to the memorial plaques and gifts, the congregation finds multiple ways to minimize the imbalance caused by their loss. This legacy dynamic, however understandable and human, can also attach itself to the changing group norms that accompany addiction.

Congregations also lose members as the result of dysfunctional behavior as codependency progresses with new and more aberrant norms. The confusion brought by the very early stages of dysfunction, and the failure of its members to make sense of the behavior of the minister and other members, negatively infects everyone's behavior. These bewildered members are unable to control their reactions and their feelings as they attempt to cope with the changes around them. They may mimic the minister's loss of emotional control, his shouting and irritability. They feel threatened as others gain control, occupy power positions, or do things differently. They are embarrassed about the erratic behavior of other congregational members.

Rarely do these departing members have exit interviews to discover the source of their discomfort. If someone does ask, they may either be surprised into silence or choose not to reveal their reasons for leaving. Their silence only adds to the growing dishonesty of the congregation by leaving it without any feedback as to how others see them. In so doing, they contribute to the "family secret," a phenomenon of addiction in which members of the family or group hide their knowledge of the real issues. In addition, they deny their feelings and distort the reality of the congregation's life.

As dysfunction increases, those who cannot deal directly with issues add to the stress of the minister. Gossip becomes increasingly normative. People may pressure the minister to be more aggressive in dealing with differences of opinion that are not yet open conflict. Old timers thus protect themselves from responsibility for their behavior and feelings. They even deny their anxiety on the grounds that Jesus said, "Be not afraid." They believe that they are faithful Christians, love one another, and want to attract many new members with lots of children, but they do not want to grow spiritually in their faith. Often Christian education of any kind is downplayed as "only for children." Otherwise the dysfunctional members of the congregation may hear something they disagree with or that violates the now unidentified group norms. They are split fifty-fifty over the kinds of people they are willing to welcome and accept into the parish. They may seek to include the minister as a tiebreaker, increasing his stress yet again, or the conflict may disappear below the surface, only later to emerge full-blown.

There is another form of behavior that is present in dysfunction and exposed in recovery, and that is reactive negativity. No matter what issue or action is proposed, there will be a reason why it should not or cannot be done. Members in long-term leadership positions will say, "We tried that before," or find other ways to rationalize their refusal to consider other options. They speak with a great deal of confidence and authority and sometimes they are right. However, their collective attitude introduces an element of discouragement and even depression into the congregation. What may not have worked before may work now; perhaps it is simply a matter of timing. This negative behavior is more likely an attempt on the part of the leadership to gain power over the ideas, changes, and new vision being proposed. That individual power move is designed to serve the interests of the one who wields it rather than the health of the congregation.

ADDICTS, BOUNDARIES, AND COMMUNICATION

The sorts of newcomers that the codependent congregation attracts intuitively know that their behavior will be tolerated and supported. Since they lack personal boundaries, they want and often get a good deal of support for their problem behavior. From the beginning, they will ask for and usually receive important lay positions, use of the church's office space, or a disproportionate share of the minister's unlimited time and resources. One such problem soul used the church copier for pornography, counted the church offering until he was caught pocketing it, and taught Sunday school in violation of his probation. In the same church concerns over a member who was a registered sex offender were pushed aside by the church governing council, which did not want to hear the truth or cope with the problem.

Since many of the impaired marginal members are experienced in fomenting personal crisis, they will appeal to the congregation's caretakers. They will find patience and tolerance as they move from one member to another, only being discovered when someone says, "But I did that for her." The individual seeking care is, in fact, manipulative, very able to make a poor choice seem wise, and appealing to whatever they intuitively sense is their target's weak point. Who wouldn't respond to desperate need in an intolerable situation, and offer assistance?

What damage the innocent caretakers do is multiplied by helpful clergy. The minister will help those who drain them with requests for money or counseling. He will encourage them to find their own niche in the congregation. Volunteering is part of church life. Members who take on tasks that others don't want, or step in to run a congregational group, even though they lack the skills and mental stability to perform their duties, are certain to be valued. These individuals are giving and they have the best of intentions, just like other members. Despite their limitations they can "do something" and in so doing, avoid confronting their own woundedness.

As fear and anxiety increase, and a congregation's impairment progresses, addicts of all kinds with significant personal problems find a familiar and usually welcome home. Their marital troubles, employment problems, acting out of children, depression, or family violence mask the underlying issue of substance abuse or other addictions. Included in this group are food addicts, gamblers, and those with sexual compulsions. These individuals also may have legal problems involving driving under the influence of drugs or alcohol, financial problems, embezzlement, infidelity, the use of pornography, and the like.

Those with personality disorders (narcissism, borderline, passive-aggressive, or extremely dependent as well as those with sociopathic personality traits) may function in the congregation for a while. Either their dysfunction is seen as humorous or "cute," and they are tolerated, or their charm and adaptability make them welcome; they are at times admitted into the leadership of the congregation. After all, they are willing to work and to take roles that others may not wish to accept. Soon they are able to insinuate their way into the heart of the congregation. However, when their personalities become impossible to ignore, the congregation may respond with a sense of betrayal that leads to a highly public split or "divorce." Their loss leaves a gap in the congregation that, coupled with the congregation's determination to view the person unrealistically ("She was such a nice woman!"), also contributes to its illusions and false identity of the congregation ("We're all nice people.").

From time to time someone's impairment reaches crisis proportions—a sex offender, embezzler, or child abuser makes the evening news. Such scandals become grist for the conversation of the self-righteous and create more opportunity for compulsive caretakers to "help" the suffering and the families of the victims. It is also a time when denial shields the congregation from their responsibility as "enablers" of the offender. Only a minister who can directly and honestly walk the congregation through this time can help it cope with the breakdown in its midst. Avoiding the publicly identified problem child simply reinforces secrecy.

Hate, anger, and discrimination against an offender are unacceptable; healthy congregations make agreements with such people about acceptable behavior. Reasonable and open boundary setting is designed to contain the offender and to ensure the safety of the congregation.

In such congregations lay leadership too often provides an opportunity for the emergence of personal ministry and strengthening of power. Individuals who are anxious or fearful find relief by being in control of their parish group, the governing council, educational programming, or social events. As the congregation's dysfunction increases, the church provides a medium for narcissistic people to say to themselves: "I am owed this opportunity for Christian service and look how well I perform it." They may be addicted people who control others with outbursts of temper, caused on occasion by withdrawal from their preferred substance or compulsion.

Clergy children with unresolved issues, especially "authority problems," often challenge leadership as a way of resolving their own sense of powerlessness over God, the church, and their minister parent. They choose behavior that will unfailing embarrass the parent, sometimes with minimal consequences but at other times becoming major heartbreaks for the congregation who knew them as children and watched them grow up. They may gain prestige, money, or other assistance by manipulating "caretakers" into helping them: "After all, their father is a minister." Since the congregation itself is experiencing both loss of control and feelings of powerlessness, such rebellion fits into the illusion that the congregational life is "normal."

BLURRING BOUNDARIES

Boundaries and limits in any church system, be they legal, doctrinal, or procedural provide a structure that codifies congregational norms in ways that vary from denomination to denomination. Organizations have different names for them, but boundaries serve the purpose of proving unity, conformity, and connections with other members of the denomination. Ignoring corporate boundaries (such as bylaws, job description, standards of incorporation) creates stress within the congregation itself. The lack of structure causes tension in the congregation's polity that developed from the tenets, doctrine, and discipline of their particular Christian tradition. The inability to discern identifiable common norms strains the congregation's link to other congregations, local judicatories, and denominational groups. A broader and broader spectrum of belief permeates the congregational boundaries, resulting in a tension between individual members or groups of members who become more and more rigid in their efforts to "hold fast the faith." Sometimes these groups leave the congregation or the denomination and form new communities.

Two aspects of boundary blurring stand out. The first is the inability of people to work together without one individual or group "taking over" the task at hand. It is always under the guise of "being helpful," but underlying this behavior is the certainty that no one else can perform this task up to their standards. Role definitions get fuzzy and then disappear. These members of the church who "do everything" in the congregation mean well, and after all, groups within the congregation always need help—"their help." Ignoring the skills and gifts of other members, they give the impression that no other groups are needed to maintain the life of the congregation. They also are people who like to maintain the homeostasis of the dysfunctional congregation with strong and firm control. In the small church they are often members of the founding family that have traditionally passed their place in the congregation (along with their dysfunction) to the next generation.

The second characteristic of boundary blurring is triangulation. Members who are not able to deal directly with persons or issues tell someone else to tell someone else; they trianglulate with authority figures. A frequent example of triangulation is when those in leadership are told that someone (X) is in conflict with someone else (Y) by a third member (Z). Another example is the "everyone says" device whereby the opinion of some is represented by the opinion of all. This information, usually negative, is taken personally and raises the anxiety of the clergy—are they poor caregivers or not really "leadership material?" Honesty suffers, while the people who find this "normal" are right at home in the community.

A congregation has, by its very nature, a language and symbol system that accompanies its self-narrative and corporate history. The use of language that is unique and attached to people, places, and things that others in the denomination call by another name is equally disarming. Just as teenagers use "slang" all the time, this "in-group talk" isolates and separates the people who speak it from others in the denominational community. It takes some time to understand and correct this habit of "slang" so that members, particularly of the governing council, realize that what they say has little meaning to others, even in the congregation. Listening carefully will not help outsiders understand; it creates more confusion, isolation, and stress, and the congregation continues its slide into dysfunction. That distorted communication also may take the form of symbolic substitution: for example the use of flowering branches because they are cheaper rather than palms during the Palm Sunday service, stretches a cultural and church tradition.

Another communication problem concerns the worship service itself. To make "the service easier to follow," the congregation may develop idiosyncratic worship booklets or manuals. This option for worship is unlikely to be announced, so poor communication again isolates the congregation. Hymns are not announced, or else they provide an opportunity for a privileged few to demonstrate their personal skills as soloists. Visitors are left to wonder what music to sing, and the congregation may even begin using its own non-traditional forms of music. Some of this change is creative and appropriate. The inability of the worship leaders to communicate the differences to marginal members and visitors, however, serves several purposes. It not only excludes visitors, but carries an unspoken message: "If you belonged here, you would know what we are doing at worship."

Those parishioners who are themselves cut off by their feelings of poor self-worth sink deeper into isolation. They put the clergy leadership on a pedestal to support their dependency needs. They attempt to occupy the minister's time with conversation at social events, with well-meant but insincere flattery, about the minister's wonderful attributes. They extol the virtues of their building ("the wonderful Tiffany windows!") to newcomers rather than help them find their way to coffee hour or follow the worship service. They view the congregation through rose-colored glasses, never seeing or even desiring to see the truth about situations or individuals. They commit the sins of idolatry and pride, of being "nice" rather than tactful or honest.

Other kinds of people attracted to impaired congregations are those with unresolved or neurotic guilt. Perhaps they carry a secret and attempt to seek forgiveness for a legitimate personal violation of the church's teaching, one way or another. Confession and absolution, if it is meaningful to the denomination, may help relieve their feelings. They often work very hard for the church and for mission outreach in order to absolve themselves. If however they suffer from neurotic guilt or feel shame, nothing the minister or congregation can do will help them find forgiveness. The neurotic guilt is focused on something they did not do, but took upon themselves blame for another individual's act or its consequences. Distinguishing between these two categories of guilt is important to the outcome of pastoral care. Occasionally, a person from a family undermined by addiction will talk about this secret to anyone and everyone, for a variety of reasons, from attention-getting to finding relief. These members pose a difficult problem for the minister. If the family secret is something that should be reported to the authorities, the situation may escalate.

Members who are overly anxious in response to the congregation's gradual transformation may be highly fearful or sensitive to any change at all, and dread the loss of personal power in all parts of life. They deflect this onto the church, becoming highly vocal and resistant to change in general or specific kinds of change. They emerge, person by person, to test the situation with ideas, communication, threats to leave, or failure to fulfill their responsibilities. They want to be noticed; some become openly antagonistic. Others bring an old issue to the fore. For example, a woman may ask the new minister who followed two women clergy to deal with an unrelated counseling issue of sexual offense "immediately"—a number of years ago a minister left as a result of sexual offenses and clearly that sense of betrayal is still present. Newcomers who bring their old ways into the church are criticized; the changes brought about by new clergy (or even former clergy) become a source of irritability that becomes intensely vocalized by anxious members. They also engage in triangulating behavior, making their friends the communicators to authority; their behavior often occurs in personal clusters. The minister, recognizing their anxiety, would be best advised to be a non-anxious presence whenever possible, for attempts to control or redirect the anxiety will simply cause it to increase.

An interesting and overt phenomenon in a congregation moving toward breakdown is the normative use of alcohol in the congregation's social life. Coffee hours include the sale of mimosas (orange juice and champagne) to raise funds. Holiday breakfasts on Christmas and Easter include lavish amounts of champagne. There is often alcohol advertised at outdoor summer functions; barbeques and picnics must always include wine and beer. Church organizational meetings are held at people's homes so that everyone can socialize with cocktails. Wine and cheese accompany the advertising of other fundraisers, and church members are encouraged to bring their own liquor to parish suppers. They may rationalize that "it's only wine or beer," but alcohol is alcohol. Wine-tasting events at the church or local restaurants are always well attended. One or two alcoholics in the congregation may even suggest creative ideas for entertainment serve their own purposes. It is not the form that the alcohol takes, but the obsession with its use at every event that is problematic. That too may be rationalized: "After all, people won't come to our fundraiser if we don't have something to drink."

Since no one ever discussed the topic of alcohol use, and there are no guidelines available for the congregation, such events quickly become "traditional." Members who plan these events easily assume that alcohol should be served and never question its appropriateness, nor are the legal ramifications of drinking and driving ever mentioned. The church has no policies to involve the governing council or to protect young people from sharing in the event, albeit illegally. Any effort to discuss policies or their implementation creates conflict and defensiveness; well-meaning efforts are often referred to committees, never to be seen again.

Whether or not the new minister is recognized as alcoholic, when he or she leaves, the codependent congregation will be likely to choose yet another minister in some stage of addiction. She may not be as impaired as her predecessor, but she will still exhibit the behavior and emotional response that the now seriously troubled congregation recognizes as one of their own family system. Frequent mentions of alcohol—and references to relaxing from stress with alcohol use after an event—and the focus on drinking during celebratory events may emerge in general conversation. She may indicate in some way that social drinking is very acceptable to her, saying that after all, their social events are normal congregational gatherings to enhance "community." Gradually the congregation will assimilate her, and her behavior traits, which were like theirs initially, will become more and more developed in response. Unless she is able to remain objective or seek counseling, she will be unable to see what is happening to herself for a number of years after leaving this particular group of people.

The telling signs of the progression of addiction in clergy and their congregations can be very hard to recognize. Here is a list that we have developed of the traits of codependent congregations and of their leaders which may help in identifying some of these issues.

CHECKLIST OF ADDICTIVE BEHAVIOR IN CONGREGATIONS:

- Substance abuse (usually masked as marital troubles, employment problems, "acting out" of depressed children, family violence, fragmenting)
- Over-functioning ("doing everything" to the point of self neglect)
- Compulsive caretaking (always looking for a needy person or cause)
- Highly dependent personalities (likely to put the clergy on a pedestal)
- Physical violence, sexual abuse, or boundary problems within families
- Sexual compulsions and addictions, or unresolved issues of sexual orientation
- Over-controlling individuals and families

- Chronic illness (especially mental illness) in extended family
- Personality disorders (narcissistic, borderline, passive aggressive, passive dependent)
- Religious addiction (as an escape from reality rather than a source of meaning and strength)
- Highly unrealistic (never sees the truth about situations or people)
- Food addiction (significantly overweight or underweight: unhealthy eating patterns)
- Pathological lying and other sociopathic personality traits
- High anxiety (usually shows up in congregations as resistance to change)
- Triangulation (only deal with issues or people through third parties)
- Clergy children with serious unfinished business with the church
- Significant unresolved guilt
- Addiction to caregivers (therapists, clergy, strong leaders, physicians)
- Compulsive risk-taking (usually a pattern of financial irresponsibility or recklessness)
- Verbal abuse (controlling others with bursts of temper)
- Addiction to excitement (often part of extremely cult-like renewal movements)

It is also possible to chart characteristic reactions on the part of clergy and lay leadership to these symptoms in the church congregation.

UNHEALTHY LEADERSHIP REACTIONS TO ADDICTIVE PATTERNS IN CONGREGATIONS:

- Constant obsession about events or people
- Trying harder to please
- Stepping out of professional role inappropriately

- Denial of problems in the congregation
- Basing self-worth on church attendance, stewardship, success of pet projects
- Overwork, failure to take time off, failure to care for oneself
- Enabling, rescuing, covering up
- Difficulty referring people for specialized care and counseling when needed
- Lying to self or others to save face
- Bitter disappointment and anger when not sufficiently appreciated
- Persistent fantasies of escape or revenge
- Inability to delegate tasks that belong to lay people
- Refusal to develop regular evaluation processes for self and staff
- Persistent projection of one's own feelings onto other people or systems (the bishop, the synod, the council)
- Favoritism
- Refusal to take part in personal and professional development
- Difficulty in articulating priorities
- Over-control, inability to let others take responsibility or let matters take their own course
- Loss of personal spiritual disciplines

These are all symptoms of the progression of codependency in clergy and congregations. However, we have also mentioned throughout this chapter the importance of the passage of time and of understanding a church's history. It is basically in the historical assessment of the congregation (and of the minister) that we find the most evidence of progression. Not all congregations will demonstrate all of these examples or show all of the symptoms of codependency. In professional assessments, we always approach the potentially addicted individual or congregation with a sense of curiosity. We wonder what has changed in the life of these church members, what has happened to the values and norms that they have had in the past, and how those differ in the present. We wonder what behaviors have changed and how that happened. The most valuable asset we have in determining both the extent and the progression of the addiction and codependent process is found in the stories of its members. Conveying our acceptance of this story, listening and helping them wonder what may be different now, opens the door to helping them find answers in their own experience with addictive individuals as well through the history of the congregation.

> O Lord God, we bring before you the cries of a sorrowing world. In your mercy, set us free from the chains that bind us, and defend us from everything that is evil.
>
> —From the Lutheran Book of Worship,
> Prayer for Lectionary 12, Year C

CHAPTER 3

THE THEOLOGICAL
DIMENSIONS OF
CODEPENDENCY

CASE STUDY: JOSHUA

Joshua was a talented, young, married minister serving a rural congregation somewhat isolated by geography. He used the internet often and developed an e-mail format for contact amongst the members of his congregation. Eventually he was tempted by e-mail offers to view pornographic material, and followed one of the links, telling himself that it was his responsibility as a minister to know "what's out there." Each successive internet link led him to increasingly tantalizing material. One day he responded to an invitation to send a credit card number for "the hottest photos," which included pictures of children in sexual activity with adults. Joshua realized that he was dealing with child pornography, and was determined to quit his explorations.

Unfortunately, the providers now had the account number of his church credit card, and from that they were able to get both his and the church's contact information. Soon afterward he received an e-mail advising him that his identity and contact information were now known by operators of the child porn sites. His involvement with child pornography, it threatened, would be made known to the congregation he served unless he authorized a significant charge against that credit card to "assure discretion"—in other words, blackmail.

Joshua continued to authorize charges against his business credit card until they grew to thousands of dollars. When he finally refused to authorize further charges, the head of his congregation's council received an accounting of the internet expenditures which Joshua had authorized. Confronted by the council head and key lay leaders, Joshua admitted his increasing involvement in pornography and his rationalizations during this meeting sounded a lot like addiction:

- "I thought that one more visit would be my last—and would finally help me to stop."
- "I thought it wasn't hurting anyone."
- "I thought I could hide my involvement from the church's leadership."
- "I told myself that everyone is doing this."
- "What I do in my own free time is no one's business but mine."

Joshua was dismissed from his responsibilities at the congregation he served. His bishop was unsympathetic and punitive, and Joshua continues as a "red-flagged" minister, which means his references are negative. Ironically, he is earning his livelihood as an employee at a credit card center and his marriage has ended. He would have welcomed treatment and counseling for what he now identifies as his addiction to pornography, but none was forthcoming.

ADDICTION AND CREATION

What are the theological themes we can turn to when stories like Joshua's and others we will meet in the course of this book emerge? Some of the most important are found in the Christian doctrine of creation from the book of Genesis. These stories are intrinsically powerful and compelling; the first thing God does after man and woman are created is to give them the power to *choose*: "You may freely eat of every tree of the garden; but of the tree of the knowledge of good and evil you shall not eat, for in the day that you eat of it you shall die" (Gen. 2:16–17). The story makes it clear that there is something fundamentally God-given about freedom of choice. We know from the case-history we have just read that addiction is the loss of freedom, including the freedom of choice. We know that addiction is a downward spiral of attempts to control one's existence along with more and more loss of freedom. Finally even the addict's ability not only to make choices but even to discern that a choice exists is lost. Those who are codependents with the addict also experience that loss of freedom and inability to make choices for themselves.

We know as well that the choices made "under the influence" by the addict or by those touched by the addict are progressively more and more directed toward trying to be like God. In the story of Eden, Satan is saying, "No, it's not true that the tree of knowledge will hurt you. God lied to you; you cannot trust what God said to you. In reality God doesn't want any competition from you, doesn't want you to be like God, and so that is the reason for saying, 'Don't touch that tree.' But I tell you, 'If you eat of this tree, you will be like God.'" Very quickly, Eve and then Adam are compromised by this argument for self-aggrandizement and pride. The desire to put oneself in the place of God takes many different forms, but the basis of that desire is a loss of trust.

When we hear the words "Do not touch this tree," we might imagine that God put the tree of knowledge of good and evil in the garden to test us. There is loss of trust, loss of confidence in God, and loss of faith that God has our best interests at heart. God's gift of choice makes theological sense, given that freedom is a precondition for love. Gustavo Gutierrez in *A Theology of Liberation* suggests that love is only possible between equals. It follows for that reason that Jesus is our equal in every way, but without sin. Because of Jesus' incarnation, we can receive love and give love to God and one another. In codependent relationships between caretaker and the one cared for, the latter is perceived as needy and less than equal, so that love often masks itself as sentimentality, as a "good" work.

When our children are small, and dependent on us, their love is rooted in self-interest; they love us because we take care of them. As they grow older, they begin to love us for who we are. As we mature, we also love people more for who they are and less for what they can do for us. There is a striking parallel here with addiction. Addicts become increasingly childish as they lose their freedom to choose and become more dependent on the substance they love—for what it can do for them.

In addition, addicts deny the action of grace and abandon the mystery of God for the magical transformation in their lives provided by their substance of choice. They take the choice for their own destiny into their own hands, thinking, "Obviously God didn't do very well, we have all this pain and frustration and suffering. We will heal and cure ourselves." We can almost hear the two-year-old cry, "Me do it!" Over time, rational responses to comments about their addiction become grandiose and omnipotent prattle: "How do you know there is a problem?" and "I work in the addiction field so I have the knowledge and answers." The choices we make end up being a misuse of our freedom. We are no longer concerned with being co-creators with God and faithful stewards of God's creation. In the progression of codependency and addiction, we are concerned only with preserving our own creation and our own ego.

This doubt and denial becomes a transaction between evil and humanity, whereby the temptation is, "Don't believe that God cares for you, that God wants goodness for you." The harmony and relationship between humanity and God undergo a gradual change as human beings continually refuse to trust. Why? The roots of sin are a fundamental distrust of God, a false understanding that carries over into our human relationships. We do not believe deep down that God suffers or is concerned for our suffering, so we try harder to remain in control and resist the surrender of recovery. This is true of both the addict and the codependent.

The creation story contains a piece of this all-too-human interaction with God revealing our desire to be like God. The ongoing reality of addiction is about numbing pain and avoiding those emotions that cause pain, such as fear and anxiety. We hear that same dilemma in the laments of the Psalms. "Deliver me from my enemies, O my God; protect me from those who rise up against me" (Psalm 59:1). Anger, guilt, and fear result from our feeling vulnerable because we keep discovering we are not God, and we are unable to continue the illusion that we are like God except through our addiction.

In the creation story, God also provides a helpmate for Adam and the two are one flesh. There is body imagery in the story of

Adam and Eve, and there is body imagery in the metaphor of Christ and the church. There are particularly appropriate words for a codependent congregation in Paul's letter to the Corinthians: "You are all members, yet of one body. . . . If one member suffers, all suffer together with it; if one member is honored, all rejoice together with it" (1 Cor. 12:26). The gift of the cross is the reconciliation that can happen, the binding back together of all people. The cross says, in essence, the same words as Paul for people who are trying to deal with their pain and suffering as the result of addiction—we are all suffering together. We share this in our common humanity, and Christ shares this with us, too. The healing begins when we can say, "Let us share your pain with you, and let God share it with you." God, who has every capacity to shield's God's self from suffering, chooses to suffer with us and does so out of faithfulness to us.

Jesus' words in Gethsemane show us the right ordering of redemption and salvation. In his passion Jesus too experiences pain and doubt—we hear it in his prayers from Gethsemane to the cross. The choices that he made in the face of these events always pressed him closer to God and to life. The potential for closeness is communicated to us in and through different kinds of prayer, in finding a capacity for and practice of submission, and in the understanding of reconciliation—being bound back to God.

In Jewish practices of spirituality, even in the happiest moments of life, there is a reminder of sorrow and pain: "We were slaves in a foreign land." Rituals such as the crushing of a glass at a wedding remind us of the pain and suffering of life. Christians say the same thing as they hold crucifixion in tension with resurrection, and in their traditional marriage vows with addition of the words "for better for worse"" and "until death do us part." There we are reminded that even though these things happen, we are not alone, for we share them with one another and with God. This says in many ways, "Now that you have had this wonderful experience, don't forget the brokenness of life in marriage, in slavery in Egypt, and in the Holocaust. Suffering is always mingled with joy and can always be shared."

The idolatry we see in codependency is a distortion of creation. The addict becomes the sole focus of the codependent's life; he or she is literally addicted to the addict. Nothing else and no one else, including the codependent's life and purpose, matter. Both identity and sense of self are sacrificed to the purposes of managing the addict and persuading her to abstain.

The resulting confusion and boundary blurring is also part of the "Let me play God to you" syndrome. In the Gospel of John, people say again and again to John the Baptist: "Who are you? Are you Elijah, or the Messiah, or the prophet?" (John 1:21–22) They have no clear knowledge of the nature of God except through the law. They misinterpret that understanding and therefore cannot use it, as Jesus does, as an insight into the nature of God. John replies, "I am the voice of one crying out in the wilderness"—my identity is caught up in God's plan. Indeed our identity is caught up in God's plan, but only God is God. God can heal and restore what we mess up, but no one else can take God's place, including the addict.

People are fond of asking upon first meeting, "What do you do?" when they really mean "Who are you?" This is a common expression of idolatry. It tempts us to step outside of what God has created and planned, just as his questioners tempted John the Baptist. That question indicates the possibility of alienation from God's purpose. The "oughts" and "shoulds" of how we live are idolatrous mandates. We see this in codependency when we respond to questions about ourselves and our feelings by telling the questioner how the addict is feeling, not us. In cases of profound codependency, we lose our own identity just as the addict loses his identity to the addictive substance. In so doing the codependent person is isolated from the reality in which God is present and thus from her true self, where God is also present.

Moreover, the lack of self in the life of the dysfunctional congregation means there is no core, no center. Priority is given to externals (buildings, budgets, statistics). What codependents do is value what they have rather than who they are. Identifying with the congregational assets is often the only way a dysfunctional church member can relate to another person. Codependent congregations are not able otherwise to welcome others with the conviction that they have something to offer as individuals or as a Christian community.

Enabling is an example of playing God to one another. In fact, enabling and adaptation are part of the same process of losing the personal or corporate self. Enabling is the effort of a codependent to deny or bargain with the reality of addiction. Adaptation is the outcome of those efforts to cope and placate which have failed to change the addict or hide the addiction. In fact, enabling is a failure of charity and a fostering of false hope. It attempts to avoid consequences, encouraging the delusion that there is nothing wrong with the addict or with those who relate to the addiction. There is both denial and bargaining inherent in enabling. We see the same kind of denial in Adam and Eve's acceptance of their place in creation. That seed of rebellion encouraged by the serpent helps them question God's purpose for them. We call it denial because the addict's behavior is perceived as normal, no matter how erratic the progression becomes, and bargaining because the codependent believes, "If I do this, then he will do that." The addict's and the codependent's suffering are minimized because of the illusion that there are no consequences: it fosters the delusion that there is nothing wrong with me, therefore others must be to blame. You can drink and drive, you can do whatever your addiction dictates, and there will be no consequences.

Humankind was given the care of all of creation: stewardship is another indicator that God trusted us for this purpose, for which we have been given memory, reason, and skill. We can easily translate that into care for the environment or care for a congregations' material assets. But stewardship is also caring about one another, our most treasured asset. When confronted with a friend who drinks too much, we watch silently; after all, it is her decision. We have no plumb line with which to measure this affront to health and wholeness. So we "mislead by our silence," as the Book of Common Prayer states. We collude with those who are attempting to believe that their addiction is still "normal" long after it ceases to be anything but a caricature of social behavior. We become part of the problem by keeping a personal secret. This is an unfaithful act. Do we not care, and are we not one way God acts in the world? We might say we are (or are not) our brother's and our sister's keeper, but that does not mean we take over responsibility and control of their lives or that we ignore their self-destruction. A middle ground may be found in care-giving rather than caretaking, by expressing concern and offering a different view of reality.

There is an almost palpable feeling of trust between the leader and the people in healthy congregations. As a result of their leadership and mission in their community, there is a deep sense of purpose in their lives. A decrease in stewardship and/or difficulty in recruiting leadership are symptomatic of codependency; there are the beginnings of doubt and mistrust in either the community or the leadership. Satan says, "Are you sure?" and the relationship between God as giver and creator, and community as the place where those gifts are received, is called into question.

This mistrust creates yet more difficulty in developing leadership and stewardship in all of its various aspects—service, financial honesty, and motivation. The mistrust manifests itself as a vague feeling among members of the congregation that can be categorized under the word "guilt." Others are blamed for the present misfortune—"the last rector had some serious problems." At the root of these feelings of guilt is the congregation's refusal to live up to the denominational and foundational norms, to live in and through Jesus Christ. We often find one or two people who seize authority, believing that they can pick and choose what rules or bylaws they will follow, discarding others to prove their power and personal control.

A characteristic saying of the dysfunctional congregation in search of a new minister is, "We want a new minister to grow the congregation so that we will have more money and more people to. . . ." They lack trust in God's grace and plan, and ignore their own responsibility; they have to play a part in evangelism. If what they have in the church is so wonderful, why can't they convince others of that abundant gift? The reality is that if newcomers come through the door to be greeted with expectations of time and money, they will know it and may not come back. They sense the hidden agenda of the congregation, its anxiety, lack of trust, and the need for control by its members. It is almost as though members greet the newcomer presuming God's authority to say, "This and this only may you do." There is no freedom for the newcomer to choose how he will relate to the members who say to him, in so many words, "This is what we expect of you." The newcomer or visitor, however, wants to be appreciated for who he is, not for his checkbook or his ability to organize the church fair. If newcomers stay in a dysfunctional congregation it is because they have found kindred codependent spirits.

In subtle ways the codependent congregation becomes isolated—separated from others in the denomination, in the community, and from one another. We go back again to the creation story: we were not created to live alone, but to have helpmates and to live with one another. The mistrust and the idolatry of codependency reflect separation from God and create a barrier to authentic community and to being the church. Pride steps in: they are the only community that has the right attitude, the right ritual, the right doctrine. They live by their own rules and have their own jargon. Nor can the church members find a real spiritual life that recognizes the truth of their own existence. The building becomes an idol of stone rather than a place where Christ can be found and mission is nurtured. Its membership and their relationship to the building becomes idolatrous and an end in itself. Codependent church members lose their identity as created and baptized individuals of the whole church. They are not able to keep the promises they made in baptism "with God's help," for they neither trust in God's help nor accept it when it is given.

Idolatry, pride, and gluttony are called "deadly sins" for a reason, and they all play a part in the progression of codependency and addiction. They are indeed deadly to trust and faith, and result in the renunciation of our personal role in the divine plan. Boundary blurring, idolatry and arrogance, and the loss of one's individuality are all part of the process of addiction and codependency. The reality of suffering and the redemptive nature of continuing to be faithful, even in the midst of suffering, also appear in the process of recovery but in a highly diminished form. The recovering addict is still self-preoccupied, and many behaviors—the willingness to make promises yet not keep them, for example—are all present and accounted for, even though the addict is not using. She has become what is called a "dry drunk." These behaviors have been practiced for so long and to such lengths that they are now ingrained in the addict's personality. They continue to maintain the spiritual distance from the encounter with grace so necessary to recovery. The terminology used in Alcoholics Anonymous simply says, "Half measures availed us nothing."

In the Letter to the Ephesians chapter 2 we read of the sacrificial gift of God that binds us all back together through the blood of Christ. The fundamental gift of the cross says to the addict, "We understand suffering, we understand what is happening in your life with addiction, and we want to share ourselves to help you." God participates in our suffering out of faithfulness to his creation. Indeed, redemptive suffering may be called by that now familiar term "tough love." Those who practice tough love recognize redemptive suffering in all those who participate in the addict's recovery. It is often possible to see how someone's suffering prompts a sponsor or someone else to share her pain out of compassion.

HITTING BOTTOM

Only when the codependent congregation has exhausted all of its resources for self-help can we say that it has "hit bottom." The psalms are filled with that sense of abandonment and absence of God that characterizes hitting bottom, such as the beginning of Psalm 130: "Out of the depths have I called to you, O Lord." Even Jesus' prayer of despair at Gethsemane has elements of the pain and suffering of hitting bottom. This brush with reality takes many forms: sharp drops in pledging or attendance, leadership burnout, depression, or the inability to attract strong clergy. Visitors to the church sense the underlying turmoil or conflict hidden just below the surface; this turmoil or conflict will bubble up from time to time. Blame accompanies the brokenness; deterioration of property or the inability to meet community codes and standards contributes to additional embarrassment in the church.

When the need for metanoia and change is evident to a majority of the membership, an opportunity opens for the dysfunctional congregation to heal. We are talking, of course, about the kind of change that is the result of grace, grace that intervenes when all freedom has been lost and all other options have been tried again and again. The power of God in these moments is recorded over and over in Scripture. In the Gospel story of the Transfiguration, it is not Jesus alone who comes to the mountaintop, but also Moses and Elijah. They all see first hand the glorious presence of God and hear the assuring voice of God. Similarly, after the giving of the law on Mt. Sinai, Moses returns to speak to his community. When he is struck blind, Paul requires the help of those with him to find

Ananias and from him to receive restoration of his sight. There is a communal aspect to the action of grace and God. In AA we see this from the very beginning of recovery when some old-timer says gruffly, "Get a sponsor." Get someone who will stick with you through the tough times ahead and guide you through the first years of recovery.

A second aspect of transfiguration is that it does not involve a death, but a journey. Transfiguration requires active seeking and participation with grace; the call to return is never ending. We sense this in the nudges and prompts we receive from time to time that we may ignore, an impulse toward recovery that we can recognize if and when we look back. The oft-quoted phrase of St. Augustine defines it—"My heart is restless until it finds its rest in you." Recovery may indeed begin with glimpses of God's glory which draw us into wholeness. The yearning may result in a feeling so strong that we plan and strategize on how we will not drink or use again. We cling to the people that we meet along the way who talked about recovery. We reflect upon the promises that we make day after day with hope, promises that quickly became hopeless when we do not take action "with God's help."

After he is raised from the dead, Jesus undergoes such a significant change that he is not immediately recognized by the disciples until he does something familiar by breaking bread and giving them fish. Recognition is gradual and relational: something is familiar and something is different. These changes are about resurrection, but they also include a death. The death may be of pride or the expectation that the addict or the congregation has all the answers; they do, but not in the way they think. In the garden of the resurrection, Mary does not know Jesus immediately, but only after she acknowledges his disappearance and loss. The disciples come to believe only after some of them have seen the empty tomb for themselves. Then there is Thomas, who must also see for himself and makes his unique and special demand, bargaining with God.

Just as the disciples did not experience the Resurrection all at the same time, we cannot expect that the addict or the dysfunctional congregation will heal at the same pace. They are changed by grace and the initial action of God's love, but it will take place one day at a time and recovery will need to be continually supported and monitored. The congregation is not going to be transformed by anything less than a critical mass within its membership. As the center of gravity shifts, and the group norm changes, those who are more impaired have less influence and may leave the congregation to find another that is more tolerant of their character defects and dysfunctional behavior. It is a similar process for a family's acceptance of chronic illness, in which the majority of the family and the "identified patient" move toward acceptance together but as separate individuals. Some will reach acceptance sooner than others, although they are all on the same journey.

Acceptance in this instance can be seen as incarnational: they discover God is with them in the present reality, guiding, accompanying, and even leading them. At a specific time and place, the truth in Jesus Christ sets them free. Enough of the congregation will see the importance of this change that, as foundational values emerge, the whole congregation is transfigured. They will no longer desire to take shelter in the past or tolerate deviating from the truth of their situation. They "will sing the Lord's song in a new land" and return from their exile. They will recapture their old culture, sometimes in a new form, and their language will no longer isolate them from their God-given purpose. The customs and habits that isolated them from their denominational life were the result of conformity to old norms, created in rebellion against a larger church authority.

One significant change will be the congregation's use of language, which in itself indicates a major transformation in the recovery process. The word is made flesh in a very real sense. For example, in some congregations marked by sexual addiction, even the most casual conversation will have an overlay of sexual innuendo. It is often not straightforward, but rather a kind of sexual teasing. This will change with recovery over the years so that the church's members are no longer hiding their fear and vulnerability behind language and sexual teasing. In the same way, joking about or referring to drinking at social events begins a similar process; the interest is not in gathering for fellowship but for alcohol. Code words for drinking and drunkenness as well as hard drug use are everywhere and ever evolving in our society to hide the drastic impact of addiction and alcohol use. For this reason, policies about alcohol use in a congregation normally state that a congregation may no longer advertise alcohol to attract people to their social event. Moreover the language of substance abuse often touches upon the spiritual aspects of life or desirable qualities of society. Words such as "ecstasy" and "high" may also be found in allusions to prayer and an encounter with God.

The issues around such crises are theological concepts and may also embody ethical and moral problems. A crisis can be defined as an opportunity for decision-making. Too often the addict and the codependent congregation are left as mere husks rather than with the hope of fruitful life. Both intervention and recovery are a matter of looking for the opportunities that present themselves: someone with serious legal or medical problems caused by addiction is more ready to listen to the prompting of grace. To ignore those opportunities by minimizing or rationalizing their severity is to keep the family secret. Jesus said, "I am the way, the truth and the life" (John 14:6)—if there is no truth then there is no life.

The prophets were truth tellers, and it is no wonder that they got a hostile reaction. Confrontation with someone about his or her addiction, or that of a close family member, will not make anyone popular but it may set someone free from the chains of addiction. The righteousness and justice implicit in telling the truth is that someone sees and says that others have a choice for freedom. Truth-telling is objective: "Then you will know the truth, and the truth will set you free" (John 8:32). In a sense, alcoholic clergy can be seen as both oppressive and unjust to their congregations as a consequence of their addiction and the need to hide or allow others to hide their addiction.

When clergy struggle for power and control as a part of their progressive slide into addiction, that struggle becomes an outward and visible sign of their internal spiritual struggle—a loss of grace and of God. That particular struggle may be clearly manifest in their preaching, which may be circuitous, lengthy, and disorganized, even conveying a feeling of agony. Some clergy write increasingly negative or pejorative newsletter articles; the pattern can be seen if articles are read in sequence. Additionally, when the clergy seek to increase their personal power in the codependent congregation to hide their loss of control as they become progressively addicted, they minimize the congregation's ministry and power. When that happens, the congregation in turn tries hard to preserve their dignity and freedom of choice by trying to curtail the minister's power in order to preserve balance in the life of the congregation. Hostile humor and teasing are intended to bring the clergy person back to reality. The health of a congregation and its clergy involves the right balance of power and goodness effective leadership on the part of both clergy and laity.

Unhealthy leadership roles that are the consequences of addiction in either the minister or the lay leadership are the result of delusion and increasing isolation. That isolation becomes self-perpetuating as normal checks and balances are ignored. The temptation to be God increases the distance from the truth and the gifts that God has given to the individuals or the addicted in a congregation.

There are two other theological issues implicit in addiction and codependency: ecstasy and a sense of low self-worth or self-esteem. The root of the Genesis story of creation is the desire *to be like God*. Similarly, substance abuse involves getting high in a search for ecstasy, for visions, with the use of "mood-altering" drugs. Through them the addict seeks to be other than himself through drugs that effectively create psychic change, numb emotional pain, and make the user feel that he "belongs." In the same way, the congregation gets its high from splendid buildings, a relationship with successful clergy, endowments, and other prizes. Its members constantly need to reaffirm their place in both the society of the world and the church. In other words the ecstasy caused by addiction is not incarnational, for it denies the addict an ability to relate to Jesus Christ. Addicts are not truly present when they are impaired by addiction.

In the same way and for the same reasons, the blaming that accompanies all facets of addiction attributes responsibility for an action to someone else. "The woman, she gave it to me," Adam said of Eve. The problem is the blaming itself. The congregation and the addict find a rationale and a reason for refusing to take personal responsibility for themselves and their behavior. In the creation story, excuses and blaming are also isolating. There is a failure to accept God's purposes; there is a loss of freedom and trust. "The serpent gave it to me," Eve says in turn. If there is a problem or series of conflicts in a congregation between minister and church members, the minister will be blamed as "a poor fit." Yet it is likely that the pathology or the health of the congregation is equaled by the same pathology or health in the minister, just as it is in a marriage. As long as both the congregation and the minister refuse to face the truth about themselves, and to make an honest self-evaluation about their gifts and needs, they will cling to inappropriate values. They will be unable to say honestly, "This is who we are."

Codependent people are addicted to chaos. God formed creation from chaos, separating the earth, sky, sea, and land. People who are emotionally preoccupied with the confusion resulting from addiction, blame, anger, and betrayal, and whose personal social norms are violated, may experience their anxiety as crisis and chaos. More often than not, the search for truth has been diverted as an individual or group becomes caught up in the chaos, real or imagined, and cannot function rationally or use common sense. Blaming is a form of "crying wolf," and it is common among dysfunctional groups who are forever doing what they can to stabilize the life raft while the addicts' unpredictable behavior seems about to sink them all. Unquestionably, crisis is an opportunity for change unless preoccupation with it as a lifestyle produces nothing but more crisis and ultimately chaos.

The themes of creation theology implicit in the Twelve Steps of Alcoholics Anonymous are also found in the same format in Al Anon, the recovery program for codependents. Here we see a step-by-step method to counteract the chaos that accompanies addiction and those who love addicts. From the beginning, the acknowledgement that the codependent is not God, but rather must rely on God's power, is woven into the recovery process. Free choice and surrender emerge as the codependent must "make a decision" to allow and finally to trust God to take a rightful place in healing. Self-examination and moving out of isolation continues as first God and then a caring person or "sponsor" are allowed to share those qualities, good and bad, that have been caused by the adaptation of the codependent to the addict and her addiction.

In subsequent steps more opportunities arise for the recovering addict to become a member of the human race, with all its frailty, and to experience redemption. Blame is no longer attractive;

accountability is inherent in the steps that require making amends. Practice, practice, practice, along with a continuing desire to renew and restore one's relationship with God, enhances the journey in recovery. Then, and only then, is there the opportunity to share that redemption with those who still need to hear about hope, setting the desire to help others in a right and healthy order.

The recovering congregation and recovering Christians heal best when they recognize their own powerlessness in the face of the chaos and pain of addiction and look to their baptismal vows for the answer to their dilemma. To promise a Christian life "with God's help" is to return to faithfulness and a life lived in the power of God, trusting in divine forgiveness, love, and concern for the whole creation.

> Open our eyes to see your hand at work in the world about us.
> —From the Book of Common Prayer,
> Eucharistic Prayer C

CHAPTER 4

THE MINISTER
AND ADDICTION

CASE HISTORY: DAN

Dan entered seminary after World War II and a career in the Navy. Like many other soldiers, he had found his faith on the battle field and earnestly desired to help other people. He excelled in his academic work and also enjoyed the seminary "sherry hour" as well as being off campus after hours with the men who were his classmates. He met and married a secretary whose father was an active alcoholic; he understood her problems well because his mother was also an alcoholic. Just about the time he was ordained, his wife became pregnant with their first child. Placed as an assistant in his first congregation, where the members loved the young couple, Dan was talented and gifted in comparison with their long-time minister who had been there twenty years and seemed weary of his vocation. The senior minister was known to drink sherry with members of his council in the office after a late-morning service to relax, a practice in which Dan joined. After three years he was called to another congregation. He and his wife had two more children before he was chosen to be senior minister in a large, affluent congregation where, at the age of forty, he was perceived to have a successful ministry and brilliant career. He was known as an excellent if somewhat disorganized preacher.

46

However, after he had held this position for only a year, the governing council went to their judicatory board only to find that his wife had been there a week earlier to describe a pattern of secret drinking and alcohol dependency. Everyone was surprised. The search committee had found all but one reference to be good, and no one had suggested that alcohol might be behind the disorganization and occasional irritability they had experienced. Dan was sent into treatment for his alcoholism, and the congregation prayed that upon his return all would be well with their minister and his family.

CASE HISTORY: GEORGE

George came to seminary single and with his guitar. He smoked pot often and quickly joined in with the sherry hour before chapel. He was attracted to one of the women students known for her spirituality and they quickly became an item. Saturday night parties included her suggestive dancing to his guitar. Linda graduated but returned often to see him. He continued his pseudo-hippie life style, which worked well with youth groups. George graduated from seminary and went to a new congregation seeking an assistant youth minister. Once he was settled, Linda followed him and they married. After a few years of marriage and some success as youth minister in the congregation, he was found dead in their bedroom as the result of an epileptic seizure caused by a combination of his medication with alcohol.

In his book *The Alcoholic in Your Pulpit* William Van Wyck makes astute observations about the "psychological and emotional soil" of the fledgling alcoholic who seeks ordination. He describes their personality traits as including "more than the usual guilt, anxiety, low self-esteem, and narcissistic traits." Van Wyck also mentions the internal conflict of the young ministers as they struggle with the "shoulds" of ordination that are in opposition to what they may secretly desire and expect as a career goal for their ministry. Their subconscious desire for a large and affluent congregation and ever-upward career mobility conflicts with their spiritual ideal of humility. Yet key for both men and women in the ministry are the importance of a good sense of self-worth including the facing and resolving of issues of sexual identification.[1] "Self-awareness is essential to the exercise of all ministry, lay and ordained."

Perhaps with the increase in women holding key positions in many denominations, these issues are less important in the current generation of seminarians than in the 1990s and earlier. Still, the sexual identification issue raises its head for women called to a congregation by a predominantly male search committee who imagine her as their daughter and will treat her as such, or for men who are adored and catered to by the altar guild.

The conflict between Christian teachings and the desire for success, coupled with narcissistic needs for approval and applause, increase the stress on the new minister. When added to alcohol use to relieve loneliness, rejection, and disapproval, the tension created by these personal issues increases the vulnerability to addiction. The troubling influences of addiction in the congregation further add to the internal conflict in the minister.

THE ETIOLOGY OF ALCOHOLISM

Other studies on the minister and addiction bear out Van Wyck's observations on the etiology of alcoholism on clergy.[2] One study by Platt and Moss offered data relevant to training seminarians in a specific area of pastoral care: that of ministry to the addicted and to their codependent family members. These are the people who may be seeking help in dealing with the addiction or the fallout from the progression, marriage and family concerns, legal issues, and medical problems which mask addictive alcohol use.

A number of seminarians in the study told its authors of alcoholism in their family. This raised questions about psychological

---

1. William Van Wyck, *The Alcoholic in Your Pulpit* (Cincinnati, OH: Forward Movement, 1976), 6–8.

2. Nancy Van Dyke Platt and David M. Moss III, "The Influence of the Alcoholic Parent on Episcopal Seminarians' Ministry to Alcoholics," *Journal of Pastoral Care* 31:1 (March 1977), 32–37.

transference issues in pastoral care and the day-to-day functioning of these clergy when, as ordained ministers, they would cope with people who came to see them or worked with them in lay leadership positions. It seems that authoritarian, rigid, and disciplined institutions—and by inference, congregations—are likely to attract ministers who grew up in an impaired family system of addiction. This comment may seem in conflict with the boundary-less dysfunction of the codependent congregation. However, the enhanced self-image of the clergy may be attractive to congregations who see their minister as someone who will fulfill or reinstate abandoned norms, ignore hidden problems, or be unaware of their early progression in codependence.

Even fundamentalist congregations with traditions of abstinence are unable to avoid the effects of addiction on a community level. They welcome newcomers naively, without any expectation that they might have a problem. The national statistics stated earlier suggest that congregations who sanction the use of alcohol will find that those members with alcohol problems will influence the overall life of the congregation in a variety of ways. For example, in a congregation of about 262 families, thirty-two people (or 14% of its members) will be heavy drinkers. About twenty-four people in this group (or 9% of the total congregation) will have severe involvement with alcohol. This group will demonstrate many of the aforementioned employment problems, marital and family stress, physical illness, legal problems, or a combination of these factors that typically accompany addiction.[3]

Years ago Howard Clinebell in his classic book, *Understanding and Counseling the Alcoholic*, noted that whether or not the minister wants or is prepared for them, "dealing with alcoholics in a constructive manner is a major problem as well as opportunity of the parish minister."[4] As we noted before, each of the twenty-four people who are alcoholics in a congregation will affect four others, leaving a hundred members of the congregation

---

3. Mark Keller, "Alcohol and Alcoholism," Department of Health Education and Welfare, 1968.

4. Howard Clinebell, *Understanding and Counseling the Alcoholic* (New York: Abingdon,1968), 180.

that are intimately influenced by the addicts' relationships and dysfunctional behavior.

The seminarians studied indicated a desire for more education and information about addiction. Their interest in alcoholism involved a component of personal experience. Over three-fourths of the students had close experience with an alcoholic in a variety of contexts. Almost all of the surveyed seminarians wanted additional information, and three-quarters of them were willing to take the time to study in more detail the problem of alcoholism and, by inference, addiction to other substances.

This survey separated out "heavy drinkers" from alcoholics, using criteria supported by the classic formulation of progression. A lack of disease progression despite frequency or tolerance of alcohol is possible for these individuals. A quarter of the students surveyed reported that a somewhat higher percentage of heavy drinking occurred in their homes than that reported by the national average. Those who reported heavy drinkers showed a statistical increase in the number of women who were defined as heavy drinkers. The year of study, 1977, was still a time when the heavy use of alcohol was unacceptable in women, who were expected to be mothers and housewives. Overall, fathers and mothers had a slightly higher incidence of "heavy drinking" among the seminarians than the national average.

Almost one-fifth of the remaining students surveyed described some of the chaotic family dynamics that resulted from parental alcoholism. Since clergy will inevitably meet alcohol problems in the congregation, that is a special concern for clergy who come from alcoholic families. Their feelings about the disease and their childhood family will spill over into their ministry, particularly if the codependent congregation calls them to be their minister in the later stages of a congregation's progression. Indeed clergy from chaotic family systems often encounter "triggers" in congregational life. They will react to the various behaviors they meet in the congregation's members, some of whom will resemble their own personal or familial behavior patterns, for several reasons.

First, it is easy to minister to those who are like us, or who like us. The minister naturally spends more time and energy with a few people in the congregation, both out of favoritism and out of a need to please people, particularly those who will like, defend, or enable him in a conflict. Ideas or plans are considered in terms of who will like them, rather than whether they are congruent with the vision of the congregation.

Second, the minister from such a family background will often deny there are problems in the congregation as a face-saving matter. This denial can be a habit learned in the family of origin. The minister's self-worth becomes attached to measurements of success such as attendance, prospective income, and enthusiasm for her own favorite projects. She may even become angry and disappointed at the apparent lack of appreciation and support.

Third, church administration will suffer from a lack of organization. Record-keeping and regular evaluation of staff and others in church leadership is ignored, resulting in a lack of accountability. In itself this may indicate a refusal and perhaps even a rebellion on the part of the clergy to be held accountable. She is not able to make her own priorities heard and loses her own personal sense of vision.

Clergy have more and more difficulty delegating tasks to lay people. The minister's control issues as well as extreme "all or nothing" behavior resemble that of an adult child of alcoholics. The minister lacks the ability to be objective or to detach from congregational life to allow matters to take their own course. Belief that "the buck stops here" reinforces a strong tendency to rescue others, fix their mistakes, and cover up their insufficiencies.

The minister does more and more, thus increasing her stress, because "doing more" seems the better part of her behavior. Members of the lay leadership do the same thing until their failure to care for themselves ends in burn-out. Lack of personal care includes neglect on the part of both clergy and laity to take advantage of continuing education opportunities and to explore areas of personal and professional development. Intentionally or unintentionally, she fails to empower and mentor others so that they can also share power and responsibility with the minister.

Edward Scott describes the characteristics of persons who are able to work successfully with alcoholics in a therapeutic setting. They must be comfortable in their own skin, lack defensiveness, possess strong values, and rest secure in their own sense of identity—"This allows the congregational member to be real, but insists on growth, values, and sacrifices."[5] The consequences of a childhood disrupted by alcoholism are widespread and predictable; the disease is both genetic and systemic. Children of alcoholics simply may not avoid reacting to encounters with alcoholics or deeply impaired codependents. Moreover, the example of parental alcoholism will not in the least deter the minister's drinking; in fact, personal addiction may actually increase despite the painful and negative example of parental addiction. These clergy had parents who were authoritarian, worshipped success, were overtly rejecting, and strongly moralistic. They lacked emotional nurturing, dependability, and communication that encourages resilience in children who have a chaotic home life. The ministers, too, had a progression of the disease in their lives that included a breakdown of relationships, parental role reversal, boundary blurring, and isolation.

In addition to the breakdown of relationships in the nuclear families of these seminarians, we find, as Van Wyck suggested, inadequate role identification in both genders. In chronic alcoholism, social life is focused solely on drinking and preventing drinking, or the consequences of drinking. The task of the sober spouse is the preservation of family life on a day-to-day basis. The children are deprived of a deep and constant relationship with the parents; all evidence points to parenting that is performed sporadically and insensitively.

Among possible vocational choices for these children is the ordained ministry. In the first place, if the family went to church at all, the minister was seen a friendly authority. The orderliness of his life, real or perceived, in the institution of the church, appealed to children of troubled families, including those affected by alcoholism or the transient lifestyle of military and government families. Second, the clergy are an example of the parental model of authority, success as a leader, someone who provides structure through moral law and liturgy, and who gains acceptance through the role of minister. The role conflict begun by parental alcoholism results in the child's choosing an easy vocational solution to internal conflict. Since the role of the minister is a difficult one, at some point

---

5. Edward Scott, *Struggles in An Alcoholic Family* (Springfield, MA: Charles. C. Thomas, 1970), 151.

in time the seminarian or the ordained clergy person learns or remembers that alcohol provides a solution to unconscious or conscious conflict. This is true whether the seminarian has gone on for further study after college, made a second vocational choice in middle age, is single or married. Married seminary students also turn to alcohol as an acceptable solution for coping with marital conflict.

The spiritual orientation of seminaries with their regular liturgy and prayer times, along with close relationships and affirmation from others both in the community and in the student's sponsoring congregation, also meets the religious needs of a student for whom alcohol and drug use has provided a false sense of satisfaction. Some seminary students, particularly in the Episcopal Church, are functional alcoholics who find a satisfactory berth, including the acceptance of drinking in seminary culture. Since spiritual formation is only part of the seminary education, it is, according to Clinebell, necessary to be sure that the student is of "sound faith." That sound faith "gives one a feeling of unity, of self-forgiveness, of acceptance and of the larger life."[6]

In particular, liturgy and worship around the service of Holy Eucharist provide elements of stability and unity that can renew the seminarians' lives. Scott, in describing therapeutic intervention in children of alcoholics, also describes the basic elements of communion: the therapist is present at a regular time, talks over the events of the week, and shares food with the group.[7] This last, the sharing of food, is a common parenting function, a relaxing way to be together, and provides elements of psychological healing.

The addictive family background of the seminarian, whether accompanied or not by personal alcohol or substance abuse, may not come up for discussion in the physical and psychological testing and peer interviews that accompany the ordination process in many denominations. Like interviews in the search process, the lay and clerical members of the denomination's screening committees usually don't know how to ask or to recognize if alcoholism or codependency is present. They are not trained to diagnose addiction,

---

6. Clinebell, 73.
7. Scott, 153.

and because it often exists in their own background, they are uncomfortable asking those questions—after all, the addiction in the student's family is "in the past." Unfortunately, screening committees often do not ask questions bearing on dysfunction; required psychological exams focus on psychological symptoms, not on their etiology.

So the ordained minister graduates and moves into his first parish position. This may be as an assistant, but with the shortages of clergy and assisting positions in the Roman Catholic, Episcopal, and Lutheran churches, he may simply be called or placed in a leadership position in his first church. Rarely does a congregation in the search process ask questions about the minister's alcohol use, although background checks indicating a legal problem can provide hints of addiction earlier in the progression. However, the individual minister must be caught, convicted, and diagnosed before addictive issues are mentioned. Furthermore, police in a small community or even a large one are likely to let the minister go "this time"; they may even attend the minister's church.

The family background and spiritual strengths of the new minister. along with the expected knowledge in the fields of biblical studies, liturgy, theology, and history complicate an already full schedule at seminary. The lack of time for seminaries to teach courses about the administration of a congregation or the psychological dynamics of churches limit the skills of the minister in managing the stress of congregational life. Recordkeeping, financial monitoring, essentials of pastoral care, program planning, and the supervision of volunteers as well as time management and structure are important. Young ministers are advised "not to make any changes in the first year," but in the challenge of moving into a new community a new pastor may attempt to belong there by bringing with her what is familiar from an earlier congregation, and so make changes regardless. She fails to see that *she* is the change, in the form of a new and different leadership. The already anxious and fearful community may tolerate some change, but there comes a point at which the new minister unbalances the already stressed system.

Inexperience plays a part in the anxious reaction of the new minister to the congregation's systemic response; that usually occurs in the second year of tenure, when the "honeymoon" is over. However, we have noticed a cluster of antagonistic behaviors on the part of codependent members of the church that surface as early as the first year. These are impulsive, persistent, attention-getting behaviors that seem linked to some pastoral problem that has been resurrected from the past. The source is usually some controversy that may signify a power imbalance or competition on the part of church members, and assumes almost crisis proportions. In response to these events, the minister's alcohol use—once social, as part of the family system, or occasional—now becomes a coping mechanism in order to "relax before dinner."

Although in most denominations social drinking by the minister is acceptable, addiction also takes the form of cocaine, methamphetamine, prescription drug and pornography use. These substance issues are kept in secret: only the alcohol use is visible and acknowledged. Congregations find it as difficult to see the early stages of disease progression in their minister as they do changes in their own function. We hear that the minister "likes a glass of wine when he visits"; it is only much later in progression that we will hear that afterward a bottle of prescription drugs went missing from a member's bathroom. The personal pain of the minister, perhaps triggered by much earlier issues from his childhood family system, is relieved by alcohol and drugs. As time goes on, his personality may also begin to change in subtle ways: he seems a little more irritable, sarcastic, hostile, or forgetful. The congregation is quick to overlook these lapses and even begins to make excuses and to compensate. Slowly and inevitably a few parish leaders take over some of the work the minister becomes unable to complete due to his preoccupation with his addiction. If the minister is married, it is more than likely the clergy spouse is also minimizing and compensating for these changes at home.

With enough stress, feelings of inadequacy, and serious conflict, the minister asks for or is called to a new congregation. Among all denominations the average stay in any congregation is four to seven years[8]; some denominations, notably the Roman Catholic

---

8. Israel Galindo, *Staying Put: Congregations* (Herndon, VA Alban Institute, 2004), 1.

and Methodist churches, have a regular schedule of moves for their clergy. Naturally the addiction does not stop there: the minister takes his progressing disease with him from congregation to congregation. Again, the new congregation does not ask his references any questions about alcohol and drug use, nor will the family volunteer information, since it is at least partly dependent upon the clergy income or benefits. Even if questions about addiction are posed to the minister's previous congregation, the dependency may have gone unnoticed and, because of the move, any anecdotal history of the effects of alcoholism is lost. Those who might be aware of the dysfunction and were closest to the minister in the old congregation are no longer around. Furthermore, alcoholic and addicted clergy become expert at hiding their progression. They may have a drink of communion wine before the early services to still their shaking hands, or find fellowship in the church office by having a glass with the treasurer and senior warden while talking business. They may even convince the altar guild to put a glass of gin next to the bread and wine to prevent them from getting AIDS from the common cup.

THE PROGRESSION OF ADDICTION

For a time the new congregation accepts what is happening in the minister's life. After all, it only happens once in awhile. The late Janee Parnegg in her pamphlet "The Functional Alcoholic" focuses on the fact that the addict *may* have these symptoms and *may* convince others that they are to blame, or else manipulate them into sharing the alcoholic's excuses. Codependents in the congregation are only too willing to participate in the denial and enabling that were characteristic of their own family systems; moreover the previous minister may also have been an alcoholic, and they learned to cover up and preserve the family secret well. "After all, this minister is a lot better than the previous one" is a characteristic attitude. Any physical ailments that the minister may have as the result of alcohol use *may* be due to other sources. The problem is only identified when certain patterns and clusters of symptoms emerge in the slowly developing progression downward into chronic addiction. Certainly the key issues are control, denial, frequency, rationalization and excuses, isolation, encouragement of drinking opportunities, and the accompanying life chaos described earlier. Taken one by one these issues fall into the "maybe" category; together, they are a cause for concern.

Progression itself has been called by different names. Eduardo Jellinek, Vernon Johnson, and other specialists in alcoholism have pointed out the different stages that help place an addict in her progression. In his *Addiction Ministry Handbook* Denis Meacham outlines them effectively. By whatever name the various stages of the descent into addiction are categorized, a few people will remain simply heavy drinkers all their lives while others will experience more and more life problems resulting from their addiction. The alcoholic will, of course, deny that addiction has anything to do with her divorce or her legal or medical problems. Clergy who have been known to be confronted with their alcohol use in one jurisdiction, when asked about the possibility by the search committee in another jurisdiction and from another congregation, deny that there has ever been a problem—and deny later that they were ever asked.

Later stage physical signs (red eyes, flushing or pallor, stumbling) accompanied by angry emotional outbursts, irritability, lateness, and unexplained absences all provide a warning to those who wonder if there is a problem. Others notice the smell of alcohol, episodes of drunkenness—not merely high, but drunk—and excuses for them ("I didn't eat dinner"), and may recognize the symptoms. But by the time these signs are mentioned and commented upon, the disease and dysfunction have been on average present for ten years or longer.

So the congregation begins to become aware of the problem, but is reluctant to sound the alarm for a variety of reasons. First and foremost is denial. The mechanics of denial serve many purposes and take several forms. The main purpose is control: control of the minister, control within the congregation, control of communication, and control of personal power. Comments like "Our minister wouldn't do anything like that" provoke feelings of disloyalty and cut off discussion, preserving the secrecy of the "family" system. They also are an effort to preserve the already weak self-esteem that accompanies codependency.

Such responses complicate things further because they are based on an understanding of alcoholism and addiction as a moral issue—it is a sin. So understanding alcoholism as a sin, and believing that the church is not the place for sinners, they deny alcoholism when the signs are clear. That stereotype of sinner alone creates many problems along the path into addiction and the path to recovery. Members of denominations who have, mostly in the past, been scorned and penalized for any drinking at all will find acceptance of their addiction personally even more difficult. Only recently have Jews joined the members of those who become addicted, due in part to the liturgical use of alcohol in their tradition. A generation or two previous, one rarely found a Jew seeking help for addiction, and fewer still wanted to struggle with the concept of "God as we understand Him" in AA, While some believe that the church is a home for sinners, others find that idea unacceptable. They themselves have often been victims of alcoholics or an addicted person.

In codependent congregations members are often unable to distinguish between social or occasional drinking and the self-medicating use of alcohol. The underlying thrust is to assure everyone that "our minister drinks like everybody else." Those church members who are eager to excuse and minimize erratic clergy behavior will add, "His doctor has put him on medication for his nerves—he's under so much pressure." Thus what constitutes "normal" drinking becomes a source of confusion and uncertainty for both the addict and congregation alike. Normal drinking may have been sherry hours at seminary, cocktail parties in a social setting, or holiday events accompanied by wine in the congregation. As long as there is a group of people doing the same thing, it is easy to categorize their drinking use as normal, even though it may be excessive use to an onlooker.

The most common forms of denial find expression in excuses and rationalization: "Her marriage is difficult," "The senior warden has it in for him," "She's working too hard, she needs a vacation." As these justifications are used again and again, the codependent congregation accepts with increasing ease the minister's behavior as either normal or as personal idiosyncrasy. They have begun to be comfortable with codependency's lies as the family system regains its balance.

Hard-core denial is to be expected whenever a confrontation takes place with an addict or alcoholic. He will manipulate the direct questions or feedback so effectively that the confronter almost believes his denial is true. The minister may walk out of the discussion in indignation or ask the person or group confronting him to give evidence for this assessment. He may also assure these individuals that he has the skills to understand the disease of addiction so well that he knows he is not impaired. Influential lay people who may have alcohol problems themselves then rally to the support of their minister. They have served with him on church committees and have "never" seen him drunk, although in reality, there are some clergy that they have not seen sober for a long time.

Around this point in the disease's progression, however, the minister's impairment begins to become the identified problem. The congregation or individual members are baffled as to why their caring behavior is not effective in hiding their concern any longer; attention has shifted from their dysfunction to that of the clergy. Perhaps the minister is seen in questionable circumstances that do not appear to be pastoral counseling, or boasts of writing sermons in a local bar, where the opportunity for "evangelism" abounds. Perhaps his license has been suspended for speeding, a matter of public record. Congregational members who drink are visited often, while those who offer tea and coffee are all but ignored.

The clergy alone cannot be singled out for "blame": blame we have noted, is not a useful concept. The minister's job itself includes other factors that contribute to and conceal addiction. These include the following:

1. In most congregations, with the exception of the largest, the minister works without colleagues and in relative peer isolation. There are few to whom she can air her professional or personal frustrations or gripes, even though more and more ministers are joining some kind of peer group or going to a spiritual director for support with these issues even when they are from different denominations. Confidentiality is important and lay leaders cannot and should not be privy to some concerns.

2. The flexible schedule of parish ministry and the lack of structured hours can be easily manipulated to suit the demands of

the disease. Funerals, illness, and pastoral needs of members and their families do not occur always between nine and five. The same lack of structure may allow clergy whose lives are out of balance to neglect personal needs for leisure and family, for continuing education, and instead to slide into workaholism rather than healthy scheduling and time management.

3. The climate of conflict and power struggles implicit in any group of people who share close and intimate relationships can drain the inexperienced or unwary minister of spiritual, physical, and emotional energy. As dysfunction has progressed in the congregation, individuals with serious mental health issues will become more and more difficult for an inexperienced minister to counsel or relate to in day-to-day leadership.

4. The tendency in almost every denomination to idealize and to idolize its clergy and religious leaders is emotionally and spiritually damaging.

Not only does day-to-day congregational life provide an acceptable environment for drinking, within the ministry itself there can be found competitiveness, boredom, and lack of any sense of personal fulfillment. This, accompanied by the sense of guilt that arises when the minister's family and the congregation compete for her attention, all can be used as crutches to support a minister's addiction.

Accounts by recovering clergy of their ministry experience indicate that all of the above have played some part in their drinking, even though they were able to hide their alcohol use and placate their family for years. A typical story is that of a fifty-year-old midwestern minister whose whimsical and childlike behavior often puzzled the congregation. He frequently urged congregation members to drop everything and go snowmobiling with him, for example, an activity that provided an opportunity to drink socially and "ward off the cold." This behavior alone appeared eccentric, but when coupled with his embarrassing irritability toward the worship assistants on Sunday mornings, general forgetfulness, and obvious lack of preparation for meetings and worship, it finally drove members of his congregation to go to the church authorities.

Before this final drastic step occurs, there may have already been a few individuals, usually themselves in a Twelve Step program, who have recognized the symptoms of staggering and the strong smell of alcohol before the 8 o'clock service. They observe the lack of consideration when only wine or sherry is served at the annual meeting, with no alternative beverages offered. They notice when the minister invites a group of members "for a drink" to his apartment after the late service, or who is known to prefer a glass of wine to tea when visiting parishioners. This small contingent might share their thoughts with church and denominational authorities, but they are often ignored until there is an unavoidable crisis; before then the minister's behavior is minimized and rationalized.

Or someone tells someone of their suspicions and someone else tells the governing council, which speaks to the minister, but no one admits to a problem. In this way the minister's drinking or drug addiction becomes a secret that supports the dysfunction already evident in the congregation. Those who discuss the subject are made to feel disloyal; other congregational members reinforce this feeling. This also encourages the denial and secrecy that prevails in the codependent congregation's interactions. The congregation's denial parallels and is equal to that of the minister's denial, serving thereby to maintain the equilibrium that the two have established to maintain their balance against an untenable truth. There is, to quote numerous authors, "an elephant in the sanctuary."

Adjunct ministers and church secretaries have a close relationship with both the congregation and the minister, permitting them to see the increasing dysfunction on both sides. They may fear loss of their jobs if the minister leaves or find that they unwittingly participate in the dysfunction themselves. Many church secretaries continually remind the minister of everything he needs to do; it is their job, and they do much of the organization themselves. Their need for control may escalate in response to the increase in the minister's loss of control; the best of secretaries can sometimes put a positive spin on the minister's absence and find more excuses for his absences and errors. They, too, may be not only dysfunctional, but addicts, providing new problems for the congregation. They take Mondays off because the minister does; for them, it solves the problem of weekend hangovers. They are frequently absent, with uneven work performance, and have been known to make up the minutes of council meetings and present them as valid, yet joke about it later. If the secretary is a codependent, she will enable the addicted minister to meet congregational responsibilities in a timely manner and compensate for his lapses.

Meanwhile adjunct or associate ministers will bear more and more of the burden of pastoral work and the senior minister's responsibilities. They may hear stories from the church members of the minister's behavior, but fear censure by their colleague and also have an inflated sense of loyalty. They neither wish to repeat gossip to the governing body nor criticize their leader. Efforts, however, well-meaning, to raise the consciousness of other staff members may result in their becoming a scapegoat and excluded from staff relationships and confidences.

Codependency in the congregation has a unique pattern that has also become part of the congregation's identity. This pattern endures in succeeding congregations long after insights into the original alcohol or addiction problem have been lost. The issues, like those of family systems, persist in the dysfunction in a slightly different form, but they still have ties to the original dysfunction. For example, years ago a congregation may have hired a minister who was unable to drive—in retrospect, probably because of his drinking. So his wife drove him on parish calls and other business. Future congregations were still hiring male ministers with alcohol problems and wives who were team workers, sharing the minister's role. These spouses continued to assume what should have been purely professional responsibilities to rescue their husbands from the consequences of their addiction and hold onto his job. But when that congregation eventually hired a minister whose marriage did *not* fit that particular pattern, trouble surfaced and the congregation quickly became dissatisfied with him.

Whenever a parishioner or family member takes a minister on his rounds, many explanations are possible, but in the absence of a physical disability, the most likely one is addiction (either loss of license or possibly he is too drunk to drive.) Stories abound in congregations served by addicted clergy, including angry conflicts between the church treasurer and the minister needing a paycheck early because too much money has been spent on drugs or alcohol that month, or simply the irrational irritability of someone in need of a drink. These stories are related to any sympathetic ear by confused laity who blame themselves for the minister's inappropriate behavior. Members of one congregation recall a minister who did nothing significant in the congregation as it ground to a halt after twenty years of his alcoholism—after he left they found a mountain of garbage bags in the basement filled with empty bottles of sherry and port. Members of another congregation report a minister who went through their medicine cabinets and stole pain medication when he used the bathroom during pastoral home visits. The feelings of betrayal after he left existed in the congregation's members for years.

Less openly discussed are the stories of ministers who are sexual predators. Sometimes these stories emerge as much as fifty years later when the young people who were his victims remember as adults the minister playing spin- the- bottle with them in a darkened room. Like the many young people currently confronting the Roman Catholic church, they not only remember but finally feel safe in revealing what happened to them without the fear that their parents would say, "Oh, you are just telling stories, the minister is such a nice man." Older members comment on visits from the minister who sat across from them with his leg dangling over the chair, in a revealing pose. An occasional congregation has dealt with allegations of the minister's sexual abuse of his child by providing a church member to sit in on all of the his supervised visits with the child. This somewhat reluctant over-involvement on the part of the congregation resulted in the member finally leaving the church and the minister's dismissal.

With the increase in clergy finding pornography on the internet, problems with sexual addiction are less likely to be discovered by the congregation; if legal issues arise, however, it becomes necessary for the congregation to come to grips with it. Usually the minister's compulsive use of internet pornography emerges as the result of a "sting" or legal initiative that includes computers as evidence. Rarely will spouses or family members report the minister's pornography addiction because they fear the possibility of legal response. Stopping the addictive substance or behavior is not enough: some form of recovery and change is necessary, just as treatment is required for alcoholism and drug addiction.

CLERGY FAMILIES

CASE STUDY: DUNCAN

A minister with several children moved into the community to take a new call. The youngest child, Duncan, moved with them and began high school. The parents made every effort to be involved with his school activities, but it seemed to them that his grades were suffering and he was not keeping up with his school work. Before the move there had also been problems with school work as well as some petty thefts, so they found counseling for him again. It became clear that Duncan was using marijuana, alcohol and other drugs; members of the congregation alerted the parents to thefts of the congregation's petty cash and equipment. The minister and his wife admitted him into a treatment center, and when he completed treatment, he went to Job Corps. He relapsed, went to treatment again, and left after a week, vanishing into a nearby community. His parents were preoccupied with the problems he raised in their lives, embarrassed by the knowledge of the congregation of their personal problems, and the questions they fielded along the way. They attended Al Anon occasionally, but failed to find the help they thought they needed. At eighteen Duncan went to jail for the first time and for years thereafter continued to strain the family relationship, and stress the minister's relationship with the congregation. Members of the congregation were forgiving and sympathetic for the most part, however, because children of some of its most prominent members had similar problems with their children.

The marital and family relationships of the clergy are even at the best of times often strained by the tension between the minister's different roles as spouse, parent, and congregational leader. Each couple must find its own balance in their roles and responsibilities. They may have married during or after seminary or, in the case of second-career clergy, been married while the minister was working in another occupation. Few denominations pay anything more than lip service to the need to prepare the clergy family for the tensions and expectations of congregational life. Each move to another congregation adds to the stress already placed on the family, including schools to find for the children, employment to be found for the spouse, plus the challenge of a new culture and ethos in a different part of the country. All of these factors require a certain amount of personal adjustment, and if the minister is also struggling with addiction, it will be that much harder.

The dilemma of the clergy spouse, particularly the wife, is understandable. Fortunately, however, the lower salary, housing, and health insurance is nowhere as critical for the clergy family as it was several decades ago when the female spouse generally stayed at home. Studies show that over the last thirty years many female clergy spouses, in addition to the male clergy spouses or partners, are employed and have graduate degrees that allow them to find good jobs.

The congregation has expectations of the couple as well. The spouse or partner may wish to be deeply involved in church life or keep a distance, but the members of a particular church may be accustomed to a far different level of involvement. Why shouldn't the minister's spouse sing in the choir or work with the youth group? Usually clergy spouses are employed during the week, their weekends are a time for relaxation and obligations with household and children, but their spouse or partner is working. Weekends are an optimal time for church events, weddings, and the like. The marital triangle includes the married couple and the church, not an easy arrangement in anyone's life.

Addiction, as we noted, further strains the marital relationship; the family will become increasingly isolated as drinking or addiction progresses. While earlier the spouse may have accompanied the clergy person to social events, now he or she may stay at home because of a demanding job and because the clergy person is beginning to have episodes of excessive drinking. The spouse may answer the telephone, take messages, and make excuses for the minister; clergy spouses often do that in any case. But gradually the minister's drinking becomes an obvious problem that the spouse sees first, and more immediately affects both the spouse and the children.

The spouse may insist, as the disease progresses, on knowing where the minister is at all times. If there have been driving problems, illegal or perceived, the clergy spouse may ask his wife to drive him to church functions. The tug of war escalates, and the minister may succumb to her demands for control because of the guilt he feels if he perceives addiction to be immoral or sinful behavior. The persistent inaccessibility of the minister is a warning flag. In addition, if the spouse is also an alcoholic, they will enable each other and protect themselves from the congregation because both of them are becoming increasingly impaired. This impairment would be evident to others in the home; the problem of increasing addiction is one they have lived with from congregation to congregation.

There are, however, continued efforts on the part of the family to control the minister's drinking as role definition and relational interaction deteriorate. The clergy spouse who is employed does not have as much anxiety over the loss of benefits as he or she would if they were solely dependent on the clergy person's benefit package. As the disease progresses, the spouse will worry instead about her own sanity and the effect on the children; children will respond in different ways depending on their age and their ability to absent themselves from the conflict and tension at home. They cope with the situation in various ways, but their underlying feelings are those of loneliness, fear, anger, confusion, and a sense of rejection. Humor becomes more a method of distraction from the situation than evidence of real happiness. It may also hide anger and hostility toward one or more parent for allowing the situation to continue.

Gradually the clergy spouse begins to treat the minister like a recalcitrant child; pity and protective feelings replace the earlier resentment and hostility. If problems and conflicts cannot be resolved, the spouse may separate from the minister, with ensuing conflict in the congregation. Parishioners may have liked the spouse or, perversely, blame the spouse for deserting the minister. In our society, it is more likely that a man will leave an alcoholic wife than a woman will leave an alcoholic husband. The male spouse and children, if there are any, will reorganize its family system without the minister; if divorce is acceptable and even if it isn't, they will leave.

Other family members and relatives will either provide a sympathetic ear to the minister and her drinking and denial, or confront her. Advice ranges from moderating her drinking habit to using willpower, neither of which is effective, no matter who suggests it. The physiological progression of the disease has so affected the minister's body that neither remedy is possible. Should she succeed in abstaining completely from alcohol or drugs, the mental and emotional changes persist; she becomes a "dry drunk," irritable and unable to cope with any stress effectively. Or she may try a macrobiotic diet, other health regimes, and other suggested cures; there are always those who have suggestions that are palatable as long as abstinence is not one of them. Sober family members may offer to take her to an AA meeting.

Meanwhile the congregation continues to enable the addict. The latest literature also notes that they have "adapted" to the addict's behavior, another indication that the healthy earlier group norms have changed for the worse. Adaptation is the final result of enabling and is somewhat akin to the acceptance of loss through grieving. Theologically speaking, these parishioners have lost their created selves as individuals and as the church. They no longer embody and carry out God's purpose in their lives.

We said earlier that they are caretakers rather then caregivers. The major distinction between dysfunction and health is the question of choices on the part of the caring person and those receiving the care. In the healthy relationship, the caregiver offers help out of personal concern for the wellbeing of another: "Do you want me to help you with that?" In a dysfunctional relationship, the individual does not offer care but simply does what he assumes will be helpful, with little regard for the real needs of the other.

Enabling behavior in both families and congregations masks low self-esteem. If you can care for others, you must have some value. Keep in mind that the Christian message "better to give than receive" seems to support this behavior. If people have all the answers, they must have some self-worth, even if the answers really apply to their situation only. While talking to a clergy colleague, for example, I described a personal stressful situation. The clergy person suggested, in response to my crisis, a visit to Florida with relatives—at a time when Florida was in the middle of hurricane season and 95 degree weather. The main point of enablement is to make the "helper" feel adequate, proving herself to be responsible while making it impossible for others to face up to the consequences of their behavior, good or bad. They trivialize and minimize the capacity of others to grow and change and find their own solutions.

> Be thou my vision, O Lord of my heart,
> Be all else but naught to me, save that thou art;
> Be thou my best thought in the day and the night,
> Both waking or sleeping, thy presence my light.
>
> —From the Hymnal 1982, 488

CHAPTER 5

THE TURNING POINT

Intervention and Treatment

CASE STUDY: DAN

The night that Dan went to the treatment center, his wife had quietly found a substitute minister for Sunday morning. Church officials brought in counselors and consultants to help the congregation understand the issues involved in alcoholism and addiction. At any given event, however, only half of the congregation attended the educational sessions. When Dan returned he was welcomed back, and congregational life was expected to return to normal. There were some questions as to how long his addiction had been present, and the people who hired him became very defensive at suggestions they should have done a better job of screening their candidates. Then gossip began to focus on the minister, who talked freely of his experience with addiction and recovery. More consultants were provided along with more education, but tension and uncertainty continued both in the congregation and in the minister. Finally Dan began to drink again; once again an intervention took place and he was sent back for more treatment. Again consultants came on board and again the congregation blamed the minister. Finally, after some time and more problems, Dan was removed from his congregation, who continued to blame him for all of their problems.

CASE STUDY: CAROL

Carol, who had been assumed to be sober for at least five years, was discovered half-frozen in the parking lot near her car on Sunday morning. She had locked herself out of her apartment when she left for church and then locked herself out of her car, inadequately dressed for the freezing winter weather and high at nine o'clock in the morning. Her relapse cost the judicatory authority many thousands of dollars because it was necessary for her to spend eight weeks in an intensive care unit recovering from her exposure to freezing temperatures. Because of her continuing addiction to painkillers and alcohol Carol was never returned to meaningful ministry. Afterward dozens of empty liquor and pill bottles were discovered in her apartment, which showed she had continued to relapse.

For the minister, the turning point toward potential recovery usually comes out of a professional, legal, or medical crisis, or else a family member's reaching out to church authorities for help or professional intervention. An unpublished study of recovering clergy in the Episcopal Church indicated that many recall with wry humor an anticipated visit with their bishop that turned out to be an intervention held in a room crowded with family and lay leaders confronting them about alcoholic behavior. A surprising number of clergy also have gone of their own volition to their judicatory authority for help. They began to think about their addiction and its consequences rather than obsessing upon their drinking, where promises to quit were all they made to themselves and to others.

When the need for treatment of the addiction arises, some mainline denominations have Employee Assistance Programs or Policies, and include health insurance for employees that covers the cost of several varieties of substance abuse treatment. These insurance policies are to the insured's benefit. The expense that any organization has when its member's productivity is impaired by substance abuse is also true of the church.

Once the help of authorities has been enlisted, resources within and outside the local denominational jurisdiction can also be mustered for the purposes of congregational education and change. Fostering recovery in a congregation that has—even if only momentarily—become receptive to change is often just a matter of good timing. It is crucial that the addiction of the minister must not be targeted as the only symptom of the disease, for the congregation also needs support to enter recovery. Otherwise it will persist in using the tools of denial to avoid participating in recovery; the recovery process must be mutual for both the minister and the congregation.

There is one aspect of the "family system" that gives an observer the ability to predict how receptive the congregation will be to change. A given in family systems theory is the "open" versus the "closed" communication system. Dysfunctional systems are usually closed; they permit no outside assistance or help. The very isolation that is caused by their codependence accompanies a "closed" family system. Each person, even the truth-tellers in the congregation, plays a part in keeping things as they are; the status quo is more comfortable than real change. Offers for help and support, even for the clergy spouse, are brushed aside with promises that help will be sought and that support already exists (usually from friends who are inexperienced and unwittingly involved). There is no real hope or belief that things can change for the better; such a system is static and inhospitable, particularly to authority. Anything else indicates the feared loss of control. Even education and information to the congregation is arranged or transmitted by the impaired minister rather than by professionals who could help to unravel and begin to heal the damage.

On the other hand, in the open system outside assistance is actively solicited. Most members of the congregation recognize the necessity for the interdependence that is so valuable to their life together; most members of the church assume some responsibility for their actions. The open system obviously has the greatest potential for successful change because it will tolerate, if not welcome, education and explanations of the concerns and behavior around addiction that have troubled the congregation's members.

At the point of confrontation with the minister's addiction, the closed system moves into a crisis mode; here is the place at which change in the closed system has the best opportunity to take place. For a brief period, as the congregation finally realizes it must seek help for its minister and itself, it becomes open to assistance from the outside in solving its problems. Denial is relatively absent, communication is, if not accurate, rapid; wiser and saner heads prevail in the decision-making process. A crisis is, in fact, an opportunity.

INTERVENTION AND TREATMENT

A professional intervention must be carefully planned and facilitated by a professional counselor. Far too often we hear of a congregation that plans and carries out an intervention all on its own. The leadership will call a meeting, chaired by a member of the congregation or even by a family member, to rehearse with the minister all of his problems and mistakes rather than focusing on the real issue, which is his drinking or substance abuse. This approach is a catastrophe, moving the minister (and his family) into further denial and paranoia (they are "watching" him). Vicious and angry meetings may take place that create a good deal of blame and resentment; they usually end without the desired result of treatment.

In the 1970s, when such interventions as a treatment option first came on the scene, they were done according to a specific format with a professional who trained the participants in their roles for the intervention. Blaming and resentment have no place in the confrontation; participants are to acknowledge only the reality of the effect of the addict's substance use on the latter's life and emotions. Included in the intervention could be members of the addict's family and congregation, fellow clergy, and friends—people who are familiar with the progression in the addicted minister. If at some point family members refuse to be involved, the outcome can be predicted: the family system is too unbalanced for any movement toward health and change.

The goal of any intervention is to move the addict and intimate others from the family and the congregation into a treatment program that will educate them, help them communicate, and offer them with the tools for healing. If the intervention results in the addicted minister's willingness to comply with the request for treatment, practical matters such as health insurance coverage and transportation to the center should all have been explored and planned ahead of time. Going home to "think it over" or even to pack a suitcase provides an opportunity for resistance to build and the minister to decide against treatment or abstinence. Should the minister refuse to enter treatment, a negotiated agreement can be made that if she drinks again, she will agree to enter treatment. Most governing body policies are clear, however, that resistance is futile and can result in job termination.

An alternative and less expensive option to an intervention is an evaluation by a professional in order to see if those who are complaining about the minister's impairment are correct. This has the advantage of allowing the minister to participate in her own self-discovery of progression as a "drinking history" is taken. The intervention, of course, is a narrative of the participants' experience of the consequences of the minister's drinking behavior. Both are important. Acknowledgment of the minister's history may well precipitate her awareness of the seriousness of the disease and begin to break down her denial. In either event, the major focus is on the disease's progression and the scope of the increasing problems that addiction is causing in the minister's life and those of her friends, congregation, and family.

Depending on the goals of the treatment center or program, a variety of options are available. Ideally the place of rehabilitation should be geographically close to the congregation so that the minister's family can be involved in counseling, while governing body policies should include the family in its mandate for wellness and healing. Key members of the congregation can also attend and participate in the education and discussion that will help them when the minister returns to the church. Someone from the treatment center also may have been asked to do the intervention for the minister. Although the Roman Catholic Church has special facilities for clergy, most treatment centers prefer ministers in rehabilitation to be together with lay people. Clergy are notoriously resistant to the spiritual component of treatment, given that they consider themselves the spiritual authorities for their community. Moreover, if their identity is enmeshed with parental addiction, their professional role may be well defended and difficult to redefine among many recovery issues that exist.

Initially, after an evaluation by a counselor, the minister may be sent for medical detoxification and perhaps a long-needed physical examination. Alcohol and other substances affect all parts of the body, and it is unlikely that the minister has ever mentioned his substance abuse to his personal physician, who indeed may have wondered at some elevated blood levels in earlier laboratory work. Detoxification is often a medical emergency: the withdrawal symptoms of agitation and tremors may have been severe enough that the minister was not able to stop substance use on his own. Additionally, grand mal seizures, DTs, and other unexpected life-threatening medical crises can accompany withdrawal. These side effects contraindicate the use of "willpower" so callously suggested by uninformed acquaintances. Once he is safe and medically stable, the minister will move into a rehabilitation program or center encompassing group and individual counseling, lectures, other educational components, a Twelve Step program, and improved nutrition and exercise.

The decreasing number of inpatient treatment centers that provide both medical and non-medical treatment is due to the enormous expense and its impact on insurance programs. The alternative may be outpatient and day treatment at a nearby facility, with the addict living at home at night. These day-care facilities include all the components of inpatient treatment and have advantages and disadvantages. If alcohol or addicting substances are present in the minister's home or are readily available elsewhere, recovery can be more difficult, depending on his and his family's commitment to recovery.

During the time the minister is in rehabilitation, the congregation should be supported in carefully examining its codependency. Furthermore, the way in which the congregation is notified of their minister's entry into treatment is crucial to the life of that congregation as well as to the minister and to the minister's family. The congregation should be immediately informed of the reason for his absence by the minister himself, perhaps by letter, with help from the governing council or local jurisdiction. Federal laws governing confidentiality in hospitals and treatment centers necessitate this disclosure as does the need for pastoral coverage to be available while their minister is in treatment. The minister covering the pastoral needs must be cognizant of the facts to field concerns raised by the congregation.

Family members and/or the governing council, however embarrassed they may be, should not be allowed to circumvent this process of disclosure. To do so would simply perpetuate the pathological dynamics of the congregation and jeopardize the chances of a successful outcome for all concerned. Clergy who have been in this process stress that the number one priority is that the minister be completely honest with the congregation—there is no room for evasiveness or half-truths.

RECOVERY IN THE CONGREGATION

Taking advantage of the reigning confusion as an opportunity for immediate intervention in the congregation may benefit the local church authorities. A meeting with the congregation's governing council should serve to allay some of their anxiety; otherwise it may rise to unmanageable levels. The governing council's support should be mandatory in the church's policies or bylaws; in many denominations, lay leaders are responsible for providing worship and maintaining the mission of the church when no minister is present. Indeed, the whole congregation should be involved, holding everyone accountable, both those who say their minister would never do such a thing and those who say they knew there was a problem all the time.

A new chapter in the congregation's life will now begin; the disruption provides an opportunity to change the church's direction and promote recovery. Many persons in the congregation have been struggling with past events that seemed unrelated and which they did not understand at the time, but that they can now see are directly related to the addictive process. It is important to provide safe opportunities to relate these events to someone who understands—a counselor from the treatment center, the interim minister, or a member of the judiciary staff.

One such method builds on the "talking stick" process. The meeting opens and closes with a prayer. At the beginning a Bible is placed in the middle of the group, and members of the group can only speak when they are holding the Bible. Everyone gets an opportunity to speak once before someone is able to speak for a second time. The subject may be the minister's behavior or, preferably, the congregation's reflections on what has been occurring during their own relational interactions. The topics and underlying questions raised can be tied to a later educational component.

Furthermore, many good films, videos, and DVDs and internet resources are available that provide basic information about addiction. Free materials, films, tracts, and the like are available through individual departments of health and human services in every state. A film and discussion group, scheduled during the week or held after the Sunday worship services, provide an opportunity to reach other members of the congregation. Some churches that have done this have found only half its membership will come to the discussion, an example of the division that permeates the dysfunctional congregation. A presentation to the parish followed by a potluck supper and discussion are other ways of reaching out to more members of the congregation. A pastoral visit to influential members is also worth the effort in order to gain a perspective on the effectiveness of the intervention efforts. A number of clergy in recovery have stressed that one-on-one conversations with trained individuals were helpful in educating and changing the opinions of the newly enlightened leadership.

The first Sunday after the minister leaves for treatment, the interim minister is introduced and available for individual and group pastoral care. The spiritual aspects of addiction rather than moral ones should be stressed in any sermon on the topic, and the need for fundamental behavioral changes in both the minister and the congregation should be clear. Recovering clergy say that too many people are still hung up on the idea of sinfulness as the root cause of addiction and the need for "willpower" in curing it. If a forum is given during coffee hour, it should parallel the information given to the governing council and provide opportunity for congregational leaders to answer questions with the help of addiction counselors.

These leaders should provide a model for honesty and also be prepared to discuss what might happen when the minister returns.

Any return will, of course, be dictated by the nature of the addiction. Embezzlement and sexual offenses, as well as hard drug use, have legal ramifications that may preclude the willingness and desire of the congregation to continue with a particular pastor. If this is the case, members should be assured that their congregation's life will continue while ongoing efforts are made to present the need for change in their own behavior and perhaps in their expectations of the minister's role. It is also a good idea to issue an invitation to attend Twelve Step meetings provided that the meeting is open—that is, willing to have visitors—rather than closed, which means the meeting is for recovering people only. Subsequent council meetings should provide a time to include an update on the minister's treatment process, carefully attending to reasonable privacy, care for the minister's family, and feedback as to the effectiveness of the education formats being offered to the congregation. If necessary, council members should be assigned to update records, by-laws, and minutes that were left undone because of the minister's impairment, and financial records will need to be reviewed. Although it would be preferable to have the minister do this himself, it is unlikely in the return process that he will have much opportunity for recordkeeping.

Another Sunday sermon and coffee hour forum can be offered to deal with family and congregational interaction, with a follow-up on recovery issues in the congregation. It is important that at these forums the congregation is given the opportunity to examine its attitudes toward addiction, consider its part in the parish's slide into dysfunction, and, particularly for key lay persons, think about how their behavior may be changed to better serve the purposes of recovery. A mature Al Anon speaker with good insight might be helpful in modeling change in the recovery process. These educational forums should be repeated at intervals to help those who have not come earlier, and contain enough variety so that members who came earlier will continue to be educated. Particular attention can be given to the inability of key parishioners to control the situation in which they find themselves with their minister, the effects of denial and secrecy on the congregation's corporate life, and the spiritual and emotional issues they may have encountered as a result of their codependency. The emphasis that addiction is primarily a spiritual issue should not be underplayed; the place of prayer and spiritual growth for themselves and for their minister is important.

An evaluation of the congregation's goals and direction for the next three years is helpful as a mini-inventory. The more clarity that can be gained in church identity and concrete goals, the better the congregation will heal, as long as they are truthful and realistic rather than escaping into fantasy and wishful thinking. Also included should be an outline of the congregation's core values and purpose that is shared in the fact-finding portion of congregational meetings. The use of the Robert Voyles' Appreciative Inquiry Summit process might be helpful. Although the congregation's early steps in recovery may not benefit fully from this positive and provocative process, Appreciative Inquiry will begin when appropriate to counteractive the negativity and illusions created by their dysfunctional practices.

Timing is essential in establishing a program of congregational recovery; there will always be a few who are not on board, but the majority can be reached with education, and using varied formats will insure better results. Otherwise, the closed system of the congregation will attempt to solve its own problems and perpetuate its pathology. In that event, both the interim minister and the consultants will have a much more difficult task finding and securing the assets of the leadership that is necessary to make the transition to health. Helping professionals will be "put off" as the congregation attempts to return to its former state, however dysfunctional. Judicatory policies, clearly and authoritatively presented on behalf of the leadership, can move the unwilling congregation to begin to look at its problems. It is essential, however, to confront the entire congregation in a frank, honest, and loving way with their need to engage in mutual recovery. It has to be done without enabling the minister to continue on his former path when he returns. Ideally a follow-up treatment plan will then be in place, and mutual recovery of the recovering minister and the congregation will begin.

RETURN OF THE PRODIGAL

Well before the minister returns to her congregation, the members must be made aware of federal and judicatory requirements that protect her employment status. This status must be clearly communicated to the congregation by the governing council. As we stated earlier, legal ramifications will affect the circumstances of her return; jail, court appearances, or other consequences may mean she never goes to treatment at all, or cannot return to the parish due to the severity of her offenses. In addition, those members who see alcoholism and addiction as a moral offense, and congregations who have previously been served by alcoholic clergy, will be less likely to welcome the minister's return even though they may not tell anyone how they honestly feel.

The congregational expectations of the minister should be explored with the governing council who should have been part of the educational opportunities offered to the congregation. If at any of the transition meetings only half or fewer of the members attend, it should be a cause for concern. Resistance to change is to be expected. Just as the presence of those affected by addiction in the intervention indicates a desire for healing, so the willingness of the church leadership to engage in communication opportunities must be indicated by their attendance at such important meetings. It is our experience that the membership of the vestry or governing council truly represents in many ways the entire congregation's goals and feelings. They were chosen or elected by the members, and they have become part of maintaining the balance of congregational life. The congregation has in many ways given them the responsibility for leadership tasks, including this one.

An early meeting with the minister and the governing council together is essential upon the minister's return, perhaps including a mediator to assist them both in gaining focus for the future mission and ministry of the congregation. This meeting is also an opportunity for the minister to share both the insights of her treatment and for the governing council to say what it has learned. This may also be an opportunity for renewed honesty and, placing the homecoming expectations for both parties in the context of the present reality.

If a homecoming party is planned, it should be simple and modest. If alcohol is to be served, that in itself should raise questions. Will the party planners provide an alternative? Will children be present? What changes might be made for a safer and alcohol-free future in the church? Rationalization on the part of either the minister or the church council should be confronted by the interim leadership. What does the congregation expect? Why do they need to have a drink in order to welcome home a problem drinker, now in recovery? The welcome may be planned for a Sunday morning when drinking would not be appropriate, but that can also evade the whole present and future issue of alcohol use in the church. Most clergy returning from treatment anticipate the first few weeks with anxiety; making too much of the homecoming event is inadvisable. Questioning the use of alcohol at church functions should not, however, be rationalized with the thought that the minister should not be "tempted" by others' drinking or be blamed—"Now he can't drink, so we can't, either." Either response is enabling and, in some measure, takes the responsibility for recovery out of the minister's hands. If alcohol is to be served, she should make the choice to drink or not to drink. It is that practice of choice that forms and grows in the habit of abstinence.

Although the disease of alcoholism, like any chronic illness, is one that includes both exacerbation and relapse, such information at this time will not be helpful to the congregation. Any relapse, early or late in recovery, may not be discovered for a time. The compliance with which the minister may have entered treatment will remain. The adage "Trust, but verify" is appropriate for leaders and colleagues. There are facile clergy who tell their listeners what they want to hear; usually these ministers belong to a closed family system. Their behavior may mimic that of the person in very early recovery or those who are not in recovery, with promises of change and small glimpses of appropriate behavior. They do not really want to abandon their addiction, so engage only in those "halfway measures that availed us nothing" mentioned in the AA handbook.

Because of the potential for relapse, having a peer mentor in solid recovery is essential to the minister. In our study of recovering clergy most said that they attended AA, and many had another recovering minister as a mentor. It may be preferable to attend an AA meeting outside one's local church area because the freedom, particularly in early recovery, to be "just another drunk" is immeasurable. That is why the need to wear a clergy collar to AA meetings as a possible defense mechanism may be counter-productive, and is worth examining with other recovering peers or in counseling. Equally problematic is the issue of anonymity for clergy in one's own community. There are advantages and disadvantages to both. The major disadvantage is that other recovering alcoholics will bring to the minister their personal problems, distracting him from his own issues and the reason he is at the meeting.

For some denominations, the description of "God as we understand Him" in Step Three of AA raises the issue of naming God as Jesus or Jesus Christ. Many recovering addicts struggle with this concept, as do some clergy, because they believe that God "as they understand Him" finds addiction, drinking, and its accompanying behavior unacceptable, sinful, and a moral failing. Bringing Jesus Christ into the dialogue with the already resistant recovering alcoholic presents him with a deity that further confuses him. Discussions of how an individual understands God—as trinity, as incarnation, or even as mystery—often deteriorates into an argument that avoids the real issue, which is that of recovery. Calling on the name of Jesus in meetings encourages that digression from sobriety and provides a point of argument for anxious newcomers.

Ministers in recovery also stress the need for support from the governing council and other authorities. They emphasize the need for ongoing education on the topic, pointing out that all congregations, whether dysfunctional or not, deal with cancer, heart attacks, and many other forms of illness. Addiction is a chronic illness in the same way, with a spiritual and emotional as well as a physical component. One recovering clergy person said that the best lay response to his confession about being an alcoholic was, "We understand something about grace." Another said that denial and minimization have to stop, gossip hurts, and "the church needs to understand that its mission is to all sorts and conditions of men and women. It must teach, heal, and reconcile."

When the welcome home is over, life settles back to what cannot ever be described as "normal." The addiction progression has so captured minister, family, and congregation that the new and healthy behavior of the minister perplexes everyone. Those whose idealism about the ordained ministry put their minister on a pedestal and who now feel betrayed by his behavior, will have the hardest time dealing with his addiction. Some members may leave with an air of self-righteous indignation.

Lay leadership must learn to give up taking over the responsibilities of the minister. Those who were closest to him, and those who responded with anger and pity when they were forced to assume extra tasks, often continue their role and cause snafus in communication. The minister will have to be insistent in defining his role and responsibilities anew. For a while at least, the question of who needs to talk to whom about what should be managed with extra care. Some form of external facilitation by a consultant may both speed and ease the process of conversation.

The recovering minister's family may continue to feel ashamed, but there is little reason for holding on to their misery. However, insight and change, acceptance and forgiveness, are more than being "nice" about the whole mess. If changes in the role of the spouse and a redefinition of what place the family plays in the life of the congregation are in order, this is the time to begin those changes.

The success and hoped-for outcome of this complicated but important process of education and reconciliation can be summed up in comments we have heard from recovering clergy. They note that "we worked together and still work together with no denial, and ongoing love and support for one another." Other clergy have helped the congregations to recover with them and also become open to the ongoing need for education and support from other resources. Certified community members from treatment centers and medical facilities, members of Alcoholics Anonymous, and ministers were all drawn in to meet with the congregations. A single session is not enough. Particularly if there are committees and groups within the congregation, they should be asked to host meetings for their committee with the addiction experts who can continue to educate and define issues in the recovery process. The myth that is the hardest to defeat is that stereotype of the "hardcore" alcoholic, complete with moral stigma. The most difficult message for the congregation to hear and accept is its own part in the illness and in the progression of the addict.

> Preserve us from faithless fears and worldly anxieties that no clouds of this mortal life may hide from us the light of that love which is immortal.
>
> —Epiphany 8, BCP

CHAPTER 6

STEPS TOWARD RECOVERY

CASE STUDY: DOUG

A member of the same congregation all his life, Doug held a number of lay leadership positions over the years. He served on the parish council, helped with the capital campaign for construction of a new education wing, and represented the congregation on judicatory committees. Working at the family business in town, Doug was a congenial man who liked everything to run smoothly. His idea of a successful organization—be it congregation, business, or agency— was that people got along with each other.

Doug's dream to be chair of the parish council came true when the nominating committee put his name forward for this important senior lay position in the congregation. As his tenure unfolded, however, he became aware of various church conflicts related to difficult denominational tensions that had received attention in the local and national media. He had not realized that there were serious tensions in the congregation as well. These tensions raised Doug's anxiety; after all, his vision of a successful organization meant no conflicts. So he did as conflict-avoidant people generally do: he developed a number of strategies to minimize, erase, and avoid it. He put his head in the sand and went so far as to belittle the people who did

84

report conflict, as well as those he thought were stirring it up. He attempted to soothe and placate people. In a couple of cases, when asked if conflict resolution resources could be applied to their situation, Doug replied that people needed to remember that they should emulate the disciples, who were "all of one mind" according to the book of Acts.

When conflicts persisted, Doug held one-on-one meetings with the "ringleaders" (as he called them) and scolded them for being troublemakers. Unfortunately the pastor was conflict-avoidant also and the two of them reinforced one another's determination to hide and suppress it. Over the course of Doug's six-year term as council chair, he increasingly took on the role of soothing people and avoiding unpleasantness rather than finding open ways for conflicts to be discussed and resolved. As a result, Doug's health, family life, and business suffered as his anxious vigilance against conflict continued. By the time new waves of tension appeared, kindled by serious economic distress in the region, the congregation had no tools, no skills, and no track record of conflict resolution. Many of its members stopped going to church.

Doug's family tree included generations of alcoholism. As is sometimes the case in family-run businesses where some kind of addiction is present, both the family system and the organizational system conspire to sweep the truth under the rug. Often the same underlying patterns are at work in the family business as in congregations. Idealization ("Conflict? Us?") scapegoating ("The trouble makers are at it again"), avoidance ("Why would we need some high-priced consultant coming in?"), and denial ("If people would just read the book of Acts and look back at the good old days, we'd be fine") all do their work.

Although Doug did not drink and was not addicted to mood altering chemicals, his codependency was directly related to the alcoholism in his family background. The church congregation was also a victim of addiction, not only because of Doug's behavior but also because of a long line of alcoholic clergy and lay leaders in the congregation's history. That is one of the realities we often see: generational alcoholism / addiction, playing itself out in many ways, directly and indirectly, crippling congregations cumulatively over time.

Change is a fact of life—not only a fact, but from birth to death a part of life itself. Scripture says so again and again in stories of healing, transfiguration, and resurrection. Change in itself is a product of creation; God changed the formless void and provided the creation with ways to sustain itself. Yet it is the most difficult event of all for most individuals and congregations. Change from disease to health affects both their religious and spiritual norms and their life together as God's people in ways they are not sure about.

A classic book by Lyle Schaller, *Jesus Christ as Change Agent* suggests using the New Testament healing stories as models to examine some positive aspects of human behavior that promote change and healing. In the Bible, Jesus is approached by many people who are in need of healing and therefore in need of personal change from illness to health. With few exceptions, all these individuals initiate the change they wish Jesus to bring into their lives. They touch his robe, call out from the city gates, beg to be helped into the pool, and have friends lower them through the roof into the house where Jesus is. Jesus rarely walks up to them and says, "Be healed"; they participate in the change they desire and in their healing. Jesus responds to them, sometimes reminding them that they have within themselves the resources they need to heal: "He said to the one who was paralyzed—'I say to you, stand up and take your bed and go to your home'" (Luke 5:24). He encourages them to see what they themselves can do; there is no time for self-pity or profound theological statements. His reasoning is simple and straightforward, well within the norms of first-century culture.

The most important principle of change in any individual or organization, including the church, is *commitment*. Those who need to recover must be genuinely committed to that change: it cannot be imposed from on high. In the healing stories change is accomplished by keeping it simple: to get up, carry your bed, and walk home are all easily achievable goals that introduce a feeling of recovery and confidence as one walks into the desired change. The presence of a "team" of disciples working with Jesus along with others who may not be aware of their supporting roles, offsets those who, like Jesus' opponents, are unsettled by the change that they see occurring without their permission and participation. The team is composed of a group of people who have adjusted to life as it is, are in control of their responses to the situation, and able to adapt to this particular one.

Keeping that scriptural background in mind, we can begin to find all sorts of helpful metaphors when we examine the various definitions of change: from fast to slow, from disease to health, from single crisis to life-changing transformation. We may call change by many names, such as revolution, evolution, transition, doing it differently, laying aside, or taking up. Something happens that is different from what happened yesterday, last year, or many years ago. In addiction and codependency there is a replacing or laying aside of one's essential, God-given nature, whether it is impaired individuals or a dysfunctional congregation. In one way or another, they have laid aside that unique being created by God in Jesus Christ. We sometimes refer to the church as the Body of Christ, but in impaired congregations that essential nature becomes hidden as its members spiral downward with the progression of addiction.

However, the word change can also mean to recover, or to return to the nature and being that God gave each individual in the beginning. That reconciling change occurs when a lack of stability and resulting sense of danger (*dis-ease*) becomes a turning point in the life of the congregation. Paradoxically that turning point, often precipitated by a crisis, is an opportunity for grace. The falsehood and dishonesty that has protected the congregation from reality is confronted with such intensity that most members find it almost impossible to stay in denial. They still recognize the difference between healthy and unhealthy behavior even though they may not be able to articulate that difference, sensing that something is "wrong," unsettled, and definitely unbalanced in their life together. An unconscious feeling of uneasiness and tension exists and spreads. That feeling, along with the suddenness and immediacy of the intervention and/or entry into treatment for the addicted minister, is a wake-up call for most congregations. Finally they recognize the need to deal with the crisis and alter their habitual behavior. They are now ready to initiate the process of seeking healing.

It goes without saying that there will be resistance to change, which may take the form of extreme anxiety and an unwillingness to accept the interim minister along with any changes he or she tries to make. The dysfunctional congregation does not have the tools or the language to even name the events that precipitated their anxiety or they would have done so long ago. As Lyle Schaller states in *The Change Agent*, individuals in the parish are beginning to "unthaw" and become open to at least the possibility of change, the fact that "the way we've always done it" may not be the only way.

Probably the change process will not be initiated by strong leadership within the congregation. The majority of its members will comply with outside authorities and attend meetings and educational forums, but turning that compliance into acceptance and finally into surrender takes time and patience, just as it does when working with the addict. The few members that are able to identify addiction, an ability which usually comes from painful personal experience, will form a de facto steering committee for the educational process. While the process itself is usually designed by members of the governing body, it is the church members themselves who voluntarily accept the need to do things differently who are most likely to make the transition from dis-ease to health. Old-time members may either leave now or later. The potential for conflict, the sense of betrayal, and the movement away from what they believed were cherished norms and behavior, are clearly going, if not gone.

Other members will raise related conflict issues from the congregation's past and attempt to manipulate or move into power positions left vacant either by the minister's absences or relinquishment by other members. This may occur sometimes in a spectacularly disruptive manner. One codependent congregation with a long history of alcoholic clergy, which included an alcoholic spouse, found themselves at the mercy of a disruptive woman who manipulated, controlled, and sabotaged many of the new rector's efforts at healing. She was removed from her position of power by a group of women who would no longer tolerate her behavior; however, that behavior persisted despite the adverse consequences. She covertly took over tasks belonging to other women in authority, including expensive building repairs and ordering a year's worth of heating oil only belatedly discovered by the leadership. Yet her behavior bred indecision and turmoil because job descriptions and other necessary structures were mostly absent.

Management consultant Thomas Bennett notes that resistance to change has within it unique opportunities that should not be wasted. The overwhelming reality of addiction and the congregation's part in it can only be accommodated slowly by frail humanity. Resistance provides much-needed time in which to clarify purpose, improve communication, assess the process by which the change is made, evaluate consequences, and, most importantly, to allow the silent majority to be heard. The key here is the word "majority." It is their willingness to do things differently that provides the critical mass that allows the congregation to begin to heal. Moreover, their voices, whatever their opinions, indicate their involvement and concern. These members have a stake in seeing this issue resolved. The different ways they envision that change suggests that they are open to other options; in other words there is a opportunity to put a "foot in the door."

It is also time for rethinking the parish's spiritual foundation and time for housecleaning. There is no substitute for having the dysfunctional congregation reexamine and restate its mission in the light of past mission statements. Does what they believed about themselves in the past still ring true? Are the goals they set for their church still evident and still desirable in the context of Christian life and mission, or have those goals been debased and secularized? Do they have a feeling of fulfillment as a Christian community, a sense of God saying to them, "Well done, good and faithful servants," or do they yearn for days gone by, since the present and the future hold no promise or hope for them? Using the method of Appreciative Inquiry, what new initiatives would they like to see in their congregational life? Whatever they believe, the change must come from within from them—they are God's people and channels of his grace.

As to the mission statement, essentially it is that part of the Twelve Steps called a "searching and fearless moral inventory" in corporate form. Neither positive nor negative, it is simply an agreed-upon statement of who the congregation is, their genuine group norms and values as they do God's work in the world. It should have a sharp focus, for it is likely that the present mission statement has been in place for years. The perception and meaning of the mission statement outlines the values inherent in the life of the congregation. As a result of codependency, these have probably moved away from a balanced and faith-directed norm to one that is distorted and idealized, no longer representing the intent and values of its creators. Furthermore, those people, in some ways, also have incorporated into the mission statement the personality and identity of the founders of the congregation.

The small groups or larger congregational meetings that focus on this aspect of their life together should be urged to communicate clearly and honestly. However, allowing the re-visioning to be done apart from the business of recovery is superficial and ineffective. Recovery comes first and the congregation's vision for their future must be sharpened through that lens of faith. Perhaps a short written survey of the attributes parishioners claim to have or wish to have will disclose a sharp division among the groups. For example, do they really want to allow children to lead worship and read the Scriptures? Are they willing to find the Sunday worship readings in the Bible placed in the pew? Even deeper questions, such as who is eligible to be baptized or receive communion, will produce a wide variety of emotional responses. They also need to find ways of identifying those events and values that have been most meaningful to them, as individuals and as a group. These are the skills and values that can guide them into the future. The congregation will find it does possess inherent resources, values that a facilitator or leader with patience and careful listening, can bring to light from the past and help them find again in a fruitful life together. Some of these past values may seem slightly skewed; they may discover that they do not really want a minister who is gay, or, a woman, or a person of color. They should be respected for their honesty, if not for their inclusive attitude.

In a dysfunctional congregation, there will always be members who want things to remain the same. Change is too frightening for them. Members may have been, or are presently struggling with, life changes of their own, such as illness, divorce, or grief. Some may even leave rather than attempt to cope with something so new and different. The reasons that first brought them to the congregation may have been the result of some change in their lives; they may be in the process of accepting the change but still be unable to acknowledge it. So they will continue in denial; they are the rear guard, holding the fort in case this process cannot really be trusted.

There will also be those who welcome change because it presents opportunities to gain the power that they have longed for; if this does not occur, they will leave in frustration. They will first give other reasons for leaving, such as the music or the current conflict. They may also make a studied effort to disrupt the change, and gossip or pressure others to agree with their personal perspective. They may also leave in a cloud of silence. Follow-up may uncover their irregular attendance at church after church in a particular town or city of the denomination. People whom we earlier described as marginal also will leave when they no longer find the permission to behave as they are accustomed. One congregation always called a young woman who came from an addicted family by her childhood name, "Baby." When a new minister insisted that she be called by her given name, and many members of the congregation followed the minister's request, the young woman left and found another congregation that would continue to allow her infantile image.

Certainly the more powerful members of the congregation will influence change. The alcoholic minister often abandons his authority and leadership to others. Restoring that leadership when trust in the leader and desire for change are both minimal results in some frightened and uncertain members who may have emotionally benefited from the minister's dysfunction. Now that the minister is in recovery, much stronger leadership ensues; that change alone will require the establishment of new and stronger boundaries. "Who does what? How do they work with the minister now? Which staff members do what?" These are all questions that will require time and answers; the ongoing conversation must include the majority of the congregation. No matter how clear and up-front these meetings are, there will always be a few who will ask seemingly irrelevant questions about parish affairs, such as the distribution of the endowment, and others who will patiently point out that the answer is posted not five feet away from them on the wall.

As annoying as this seems, just the action of asking and answering helps foster direct communication and offers an opportunity to pose the larger question: "How can we best find out what is happening in the congregation?" Leadership that responds with good communication, compassion, and patience is invaluable in managing the recovery process.

As we noted earlier, structure reduces anxiety. Good communication that uses a variety of media to inform the congregation supports their growth in each new step. Put simply, if only a few in the congregation know how to use computer technology, newsletters and announcements would be the media of choice. When individuals and their norms and ideals are respected, their suggestions considered and acknowledged, the result is a feeling of safety and value in the community. Consensus, established with the help of trusted leaders who respect even those who object to a necessary change, is more likely to appeal to even the resistant members in the congregation. These marginal members must experience relationships that are supportive and consistent with their values and with Christian values. Attentive leadership that takes the time to hear their concerns, some of which are legitimate, will advance the aspects of needed change. The goal that we hope to achieve is found in the Twelve Steps' adaptation of the Prayer of St. Francis of Assisi, a version of the prayer that emphasizes self-actualization and compassion, maintaining the individuality of each member without losing the collaborative nature of the congregational life.

> Lord, make me a channel of thy peace,
>   that where there is hatred, I may bring love;
>   that where there is wrong, I may bring the spirit
>   of forgiveness;
>   that where there is discord, I may bring harmony;
>   that where there is error, I may bring truth;
>   that where there is doubt, I may bring faith;
>   that where there is despair, I may bring hope;
>   that where there are shadows, I may bring light;
>   that where there is sadness, I may bring joy.
> Lord, grant that I may seek rather to comfort

than to be comforted;
to understand, than to be understood;
to love, than to be loved.
For it is by self-forgetting that one finds.
It is by forgiving that one is forgiven.
It is by dying that one awakens to Eternal Life.[1]

We have talked about change in the person of the minister and in the dysfunctional congregation, as well as about differences in interaction and behavior with one another, but we have not examined the change in terms of the ultimate recovery goals for the dysfunctional system. We have talked about change in terms of moving from dysfunction to health, but not in terms of becoming spiritually healthy.

Both individuals and the congregation have encountered this time of crisis and the opportunities it brings, and one of those opportunities is to take another look at their faith. Church membership is not solely rooted in Christian doctrine and companionship, nor in problematic family systems, but as Dietrich Bonhoeffer wrote in *Testament to Freedom*, in a life that has encountered Jesus Christ. In his book *Addiction and Grace* Gerald May describes grace not as a one-time event, once offered, but as part of a deeper spiritual journey. The Twelve Steps are quite clear about the need to change and adopt a lifestyle of spiritual health. Step Ten is about ongoing grace, forgiveness, and redemption; it involves a lifetime of change. It requires a daily willingness to pray for those changes to take place in an individual life, and daily forgiveness in the life of the congregation. For as long as relationships are restricted to church social gatherings, assisted by alcohol, or are marked and stained by addiction, the lifelong journey of real grace and real change is impossible. Change in dysfunctional congregations may mean deepening spiritual life beyond superficial beliefs and sentimental piety. This process will take both prayer and a new insight into the cross and resurrection; the entire Paschal mystery must be central.

---

1. Alcoholics Anonymous, *Twelve Steps and Twelve Traditions* (New York: Alcoholics Anonymous World Services, 1981), 99.

CASE STUDY: SARAH

Sarah was a minister in a large congregation. She and her husband had been married a short time—a second marriage for her, as her former husband had died suddenly of a heart attack several years before. The second spouse had been a member of her congregation, and began to date her about a year after her husband's death: they married a few months later. She was fun at a party: they were invited to members' homes often, where Sarah would let her hair down and play the piano to entertain others. Although her second husband did not mind living in the same church rectory where she had lived with her first husband, he did mind her insistence that she could write better sermons if she sat at the local bar and talked to the regulars while she got ideas. Increasingly, he noticed, she had too much to drink and he was not sure what medication she took for her migraine headaches. Sarah said her doctor had prescribed the pills and that sometimes her counseling work with members of her congregation gave her bad headaches. She also received strange phone calls from time to time, with frequent hang-ups when he answered the telephone, but she could always explain everything to his satisfaction.

Things came to a head when the church's governing council wanted to cut her salary because church attendance had declined and they claimed they could not afford a full-time clergy person any longer. Sarah began to look for a full-time job. Her drinking increased because, she told him, the stress of job-hunting gave her more frequent and debilitating headaches. One morning he was barely able to waken her and had to rush her to the hospital, where a detailed medical history uncovered not only a dependence on alcohol but also on prescription drugs, and she was sent into treatment. It turned out that Sarah had convinced four different physicians to treat her for her "headaches" and was filling prescriptions at four separate pharmacies. As her addiction progressed, her work performance suffered for some time, but because she used prescription medication rather than illegal drugs, she was able to hide it.

Several denominations have recovering clergy groups and/or treatment centers. Because clergy are expected to be professional and proficient in spiritual matters, they are often the most resistant to treatment and accepting professional help. Although times have changed, we have met clergy who were divorced as a result of their addiction and whose governing body refused to permit them to continue in their positions. We have had other clergy contact us in anguish because they cannot stay sober, and their governing body is determined to force them to resign or retire. Church policies regarding a return to ministry must be stated with clear stipulations and understandable consequences. They will be different depending on what the addiction is: sex offenders and those with other legal issues may not be appropriately returned to the congregation. We would hope that the policies, however stringent, would be more compassionate than some we have heard about, which have left aging clergy sexual predators homeless, without pension or healthcare benefits, pariahs in their communities.

About two-thirds of the clergy we studied knew they needed to get help for their substance abuse. That self-awareness, in addition to a nudge from family or concerned others, is usually enough to encourage them to enter a treatment program. They accept the reality that their lives and the lives of their congregations are indeed unmanageable and make a commitment to recovery. But there are also clergy who comply with the nudge as far as beginning to get treatment, but never really intend to continue with counseling and a Twelve Step program. Those clergy who deny the problem of addiction and refuse to accept treatment according to governing body policies are terminated. Of those clergy who comply (going into treatment with an attitude of denial and only superficial willingness), some will relapse and others will gradually move toward accepting their need for recovery. Treatment outcomes vary, but there is no evidence that the addict has to *want* to enter treatment for an outcome to be successful. It is expected that the minister will continue in counseling, avail himself of self-help groups, and have a mentor or sponsor familiar with the recovery process to reinforce the treatment's education and counseling components.

In addition, the spouse or partner and family members should also seek counseling and an appropriate Twelve Step program such as Al Anon. As noted previously, clergy spouses of earlier decades experienced fear and anxiety over the financial and housing insecurity that accompanies the progression of the addiction; a number of wives said they would be left with nothing if something happened to their husbands. That is currently less of an issue, but it could still have a devastating effect on their financial security, especially if there are young children still at home. Depending on the severity of the addiction, the spouse may prefer to move out; if the clergy person becomes increasingly out of control it may result in legal problems that reverberate throughout the church and wider community. The congregation should, however, give the family plenty of time for relocation, trying in every way to be hospitable; after all the same tragedy that is overtaking the congregation and the minister is overtaking them, too.

Children are silent and often very frightened witnesses to their parent's addiction. We have seen young children attend AA meetings with their parent trying in a mature manner to understand and sometimes protect their mother or father from what is taking place. They are aware of the tension in the family, but often understand only bits and pieces of what has been happening. Normally treatment centers will involve them in the recovery process with art or play therapy. Just the simple understanding that other children have this problem with their parents helps clear the air. It is naive to assume that very young children do not understand that when Daddy "smells funny" or "acts weird," something is wrong. If addiction is carefully explained to them, they often become forgiving and caring children; the main concern is that they will be forced to grow up too quickly and lose their childhood to the codependency which is entrapping them. Such children often choose roles of hero, lost child, or clown, among others, but underneath their behavior they are frightened and lonely. They may also misbehave to get the attention and care they are missing while the other parent is preoccupied with the addiction.

The minister will also have to deal with the disbelief of those parishioners who still can't comprehend that their minister is an alcoholic, or cannot understand why he cannot have "just one drink," and still others who will sidle up with non-alcoholic beverages to be "helpful." All of these people must be addressed firmly and directly; triangulation and gossip can no longer be a part of the congregation's (or the minister's) mode of communication. On the other hand, the congregation will quickly resent a minister who preaches weekly on his recovery and the Twelve Steps; such self-disclosure in the pulpit is generally inappropriate.

The minister needs not only to acknowledge the fact of her addiction to herself, but to members of the congregation, no matter what stage she is in when accepting her recovery. Each time in the coming years, if and when the minister searches for a new congregation, she will face the stigma of addiction. This results in a constant internal struggle for the minister who must confront the question of whether to reveal to a search committee that she is a recovering alcoholic. Even more of a stigma exists when the minister is a woman in recovery; for many church people, it goes against the grain. Clergy also have the understandable concern of being recognized at AA meetings; small towns and local recovery groups know the members of their community well, and sooner or later the truth will come out. She will also draw the attention of members of the recovery group itself, both those who do not want to be reminded of religion because of old antagonisms and those who, for other reasons, welcome God's action in their lives. The minister is entitled to anonymity on that level.

We have already said that recovery raises the issue of who is to be in charge, both for minister and congregation. Because the polity of denominations varies, cooperation with lay members over questions of authority, control, and expectations of their leadership is not uniform from denomination to denomination or even from one congregation to another in the same denomination. So eventually the minister must come to a conclusion that faithfulness and faithfulness alone is the solution to his dilemma. The trappings of superficial religion must give way to an ever-deepening spirituality, and it will raise in turn the spiritual question of surrender to God's will.

All too often Christians behave in the way described by Bernard of Clairvaux, the twelfth-century theologian and mystic, as "loving God for our own sake."[2] The busyness of their lives may,

---

2. Gregory Fruehwirth, *Words for Silence* (London: SPCK, 2008), 3.

however, after a time of activity and self-centeredness, accompanied by a passion both to fix others and play God to them, yield to new and more focused spiritual life. The congregation, the minister and individuals within it, may yearn for a more fulfilling life and make a resolve to turn their ministries over to God's care. Then they will experience something new: the driven-ness and the superficial focus of their lives will be transformed by the simple act of surrender of themselves and of others to God's care. They will begin to heal.

The minister, despite treatment, will experience a number of ups and downs in his personal recovery. Problems with sleep, memory, and behavior will complicate his personal relationships. In the first few years strong efforts to control situations rather than participate in their solution will characterize his leadership. Problems with intimacy will occur regularly. Under stress, his "Jekyll and Hyde" personality may be more pronounced, and he will want to deny how impaired he has been and, to a large degree, still is. Rigorous honesty will be difficult: truth is valued, but dishonesty can take many forms. Certain patterns—the desire to have "just one drink," the promises made and not kept, the refrain of "I can do it myself"—are still intact in early recovery and have a life of their own—"I can miss just one meeting" or "I will call my sponsor tomorrow." Communication will be defensive or rationalized, and a sense of proportion is missing. When someone is addicted, more (of anything) is always better.

As time passes and recovery becomes easier in terms of everyday living, the minister will want to examine the ways in which she interacts with the congregation, her family, and with colleagues and friends. How does she encourage or discourage their dis-ease? Does she play favorites now, or respond appropriately to members who had felt ignored in the past? Does she pay attention to those administrative tasks and details that indicate her general attitude toward her responsibilities in ministry? The life of the congregation is as much embodied in the details of administration as it is in the details of worship. A self-evaluation can be done in many different ways as long as the minister is willing to listen and to be unfailingly honest with a mentor or supervisor.

Self-evaluation raises for the minister the many ways she both fails to serve, and serves well, in her ministry. For a time there will be feelings of guilt that will be proportional to the amount of control she thought she had over her personal life; only after years have passed will she fully recognize her own powerlessness over the disease. Risking a Fourth and Fifth Step with a trusted colleague will lead her into insights about her behavior and the ways she colludes with others to perpetuate her dysfunction and that of the congregation. Acceptance of forgiveness and relief of her guilt may be uncertain at first. The personal changes she will make are those that are accompanied by the willingness to accept God's help. Her days as a Lone Ranger, isolated from the real support of community and family, are over as long as she is willing to explore new behaviors. Alcoholic Anonymous describes this willingness, along with a foundation of a deep spiritual yearning, as the key that opens the door to recovery.

It is not surprising that, after identifying the need for new ways of thinking and believing, the superficial spiritual and emotional life of the past that accompanied the minister's addiction can change again with God's help. The stumbling block for clergy and congregation alike is simply that the minister considers himself an authority on God, and the congregation has accepted that false image. Recovery is faith in action. Reconciliation with others who have been harmed by the minister's addiction will require tact and courage. There may be some situations and relationships that cannot be restored, but a willingness on the part of the minister in making the attempt with an apology and honest conversation is imperative. The Ninth Step notes that making these amends requires discernment on the minister's part; such efforts may work for some but injure others, and violate the dictates of confidentiality.

Recovery proceeds over months and years, one day at a time. It is easy from time to time to forget the principles that guided the minister to recovery from the beginning. Therefore, a regular daily discipline, based on the ancient spiritual practice of self-examination, to maintain and monitor healthy or not so healthy behavior, is essential. Within the treatment process, prayer, meditation, continuing education, and follow-up is vital. Spirituality takes on a life apart from and yet within the professional purview of the minister in preaching, teaching, and pastoral care. This also becomes another step in the surrender of the will to God. Slowly the spiritual awakening continues along with a foundation of willingness and honesty in all relationships: family, friends, and congregation. The isolation of the minister caused by the addiction begins to break down, and he becomes involved in the church in a new and healthy way.

> Increase in us true religion; nourish us with all goodness, and bring forth in us the fruit of good works.
>
> —From the Book of Common Prayer, Proper 17

CHAPTER 7

RETURN AND NEW BEGINNINGS

CASE STUDY: MOLLY

Molly has been in recovery for five years. An assistant in a large congregation when she was sent to treatment, she believes that five years into recovery she is doing well. Those first years were an important foundation for her future. She had all the usual questions—when to tell her new congregation about her alcoholism, what to do if invited for dinner and offered alcohol, and how to find a support system in her new community. Molly has a mentor who is also a recovering minister, goes to AA meetings twice a week and more often when stressed, refuses to overwork, and sets limits on meetings and other demands on her time. Church members are aware of her disease on a need-to-know basis. Her family is supportive and her husband confronts her gently if she begins to go backward instead of forward. She believes that AA works, and is convinced that a return to the drinking and rebellious behavior of her seminary days would also be a return to dysfunctional behavior. The congregation is a relatively healthy one that is also willing to work on becoming more honest and faithful.

As we noted in the chapter on change, building trust with and among those who will formulate the changes in the minister's behavior and congregational life is vital. Transformation must come from within the minister and the congregation: only gradually will the negative behavior, attitudes, and self-image change. There are necessary tasks to be done in alleviating the fear and anxiety over what is "old," what is "new," and what is "borrowed" from others who are ahead of them in recovery. Relapse is possible—addiction is a chronic illness. The identified patient is being returned to a system that participated in her addiction, and this will cause everyone anxiety and discomfort. Congregational members will be watching her, and their recovery will be impaired as long as their focus is the minister.

Our study of recovering clergy returning to their congregation discovered that after their recovery began, many remained in that particular church for only two to four years. One reason for this might be inadequate recovery on the part of a codependent congregation. As one minister said, "I want to keep getting well and they don't." Members persist in their old behavior; they serve alcohol without alternative beverages at church functions, gossip about their concerns rather than communicating openly and directly, and hide their attitude towards alcoholism. Nevertheless, the church members should never be blamed for a relapse; the minister, and the minister alone, is responsible for his choices and his recovery.

Building trust happens one group at a time, and it begins with the governing body of the congregation. Since at least some of them are long-term leaders, their assistance and networking with other members is invaluable. There will undoubtedly be those who want to terminate the minister, but the policies of the national church's governing body should preclude that drastic step. In reality, apart from the ethical issues involved, the costs alone of the rehabilitation and restoration of a trained minister make his return to the congregation important.

Their leader's fall from grace, no matter what kind of addiction is involved, raises another issue for the codependent congregation as it begins its recovery, and that is the dynamics of betrayal. It is often that sense of betrayal that keeps the congregation as a whole, and individuals within it, stuck in their recovery. Betrayal is more than denial, although it often is accompanied by it. When people have believed and trusted the person who has betrayed them; the anger and disgust both at themselves and at their betrayer can last a long time. As we mentioned earlier, there are those in the church who naively and far too readily put the minister on a pedestal. The situation is complicated by the betrayer's characteristic response, which is to minimize and rationalize her actions; she will try to make what she has done seem almost reasonable. But the optimum move toward healing on the part of the minister is to announce her part in the addiction process and make amends to the congregation. While most congregations over time will accept the minister's alcoholism, offenses such as embezzlement, pornography, and illegal drug use are much more likely to increase a sense of outrage and betrayal and lead to the departure of the minister.

The issue of trust is more difficult with those in the congregation who experience the strongest degree of betrayal. He let them down, they counted on him, and now he has changed his behavior. He is not the minister they hired and befriended—never mind that he is getting well. The blaming and guilt will remain as long as the minister is perceived as not sufficiently caring, accountable, or remorseful. A sense of betrayal begins to heal only when members discover that they are not alone in their feelings. The conspiracy of silence that emerges in a congregation does so for different reasons. Some understand the nature of the "family secret" that accompanies addiction; others fear the power of the betrayer or their peers' response to any revelation of the real situation. Still others are truly innocent; they do not know what is happening for a variety of reasons, and if they hear rumors, they are optimistic and hopeful that the talk is merely gossip. However, when the secret is out, there will be people who say they knew it all along, those who are genuinely surprised, and those who hope the minister will take the opportunity to make genuine personal changes.

As the congregation is confronted with its denial, some members begin to take responsibility for bringing justice and a sense of accountability into the community's life. They may have already been to the church authorities, organized an intervention with trained assistance, had an audit performed, and done what is necessary to restore healthy group norms in the congregation. These are the members with enough personal strength to make a decision in favor of health. There will be another group of members who were attracted to the congregation precisely because of its dysfunction; they are not psychologically strong enough to make decisions. They may go along with everyone else or, if they feel sufficiently threatened by the idea of change, attempt to sabotage the church's healing in unconscious ways. This is how they behave in other aspects of their lives and other relationships, so it will gratify them personally to continue this behavior. They are unable to see that this is the time to put God first, and to believe that God's power can restore the sanity and reality of their life in Christian community.

The first step in congregational recovery before and after the minister returns, which is also part of dealing with the sense of betrayal, is to challenge the false self-image that the congregation has incorporated into its life. Their expectations of themselves are unrealistic, as are their expectations of their minister, and that realization may lead to outbursts of anger. They are not the biggest, best, wealthiest, most historic, most "reaching-out" church in the world—nor are they the poorest, the most victimized, the least cared for. The emotional inflation and subsequent depression that accompanies addiction is also part of their dysfunction, as they will acknowledge in excusing and compensating for their feelings of poor self-worth.

To insist on the reestablishment of boundaries, bylaws, and adherence to denominational identity and norms as part of recovery is essential in introducing reality into the church's life. Now the congregation's common life and new beginning depends on structure and transparency. Services begin on time, schedules are established and followed, job descriptions are adhered to. This is a time for cleaning up and putting in place those tasks that are administratively necessary but have been neglected by both minister and congregation. In this process the distribution of power in the congregation ideally moves toward congruence between the extrinsic (visible) leader and intrinsic (invisible) leadership.

Basic record-keeping and maintenance also help the church return to a semblance of order after being neglected by both minister and congregation. Financial records are audited; policies that require this by the governing body are appropriate. Criteria for book-keeping should include a description of items that are beyond the range of the governing body norms. Ambiguous or misleading titles for the different parish funds (such as "the Flower Fund") need to be cleared up and redone. It is important that committees meet, agendas are clear, bylaws are followed, and rules and regulations are adhered to stringently. Plans for education and congregational recovery must be made by those who understand that this organization is vital to their survival as a church. Mission statements should be revisited and stewardship rethought and refocused after a realistic assessment of the congregation's life together. Yearly opportunities for education and evaluation of key roles in leadership can be put in place.

Everywhere throughout the congregation, boundaries are established that reduce anxiety and solidify the new change. A variety of announcements, newsletters, posters, and events are used to convey decisions made by lay leaders. The most important information to be distributed is that found in financial statements and the minutes of meetings, as mundane as it may seem; the message such disclosure conveys is one of both responsibility and transparency about finances and leadership. Accountability on everyone's part is a necessity, from stewardship and church attendance to schedules for young people's meetings. Often the people who control the communication have the power to help or hinder healing. The use of language, the content, and the frequency of communication eliminate the fantasy and guess work of dysfunction.

Interpersonal relationships and behaviors must also change. Truth-telling rather than "being nice," tactful confrontation, begins the healing of those members who contributed to the dysfunctional behavior in the first place. As Episcopal priest Sam Shoemaker pointed out long ago in *What The Church can learn from Alcoholics Anonymous*, small groups are the foundation of Alcoholics Anonymous, and the result of individual willingness to accept the frailty of humanity rather than to maintain a mask of Christian perfection. (Mega-churches also understand the healing intimacy of the small group.) This kind of redemptive acceptance leads to a healthier community and church. The "gag rule" that bound the congregation to denial yields to conversation that builds support and friendships.

Congregations should expect to make similar changes based on what they have learned from educational initiatives and programs such as Appreciative Inquiry, which will help them to focus on positive assets, communication, and other aspects of their corporate life. Congregations too can have low self-esteem. Lack of maintenance, poor stewardship, and over-dependence on an endowment indicates more graphically than any words can say that they believe their contribution as individuals is of little value. Sermons on discipleship and God's gifts to them, programs on prayer, examination of outreach efforts, all contribute to the reality that these Christians do have much to offer the church and the world.

Another option to assist their recovery would be the use of a survey to help the minister and others become fully aware of the needs within the membership that have arisen from its adaptation to addiction. The survey may indicate a need for lay pastoral leadership as well as clergy leadership to provide resources and support to members so affected. Awareness of the seriousness of the issue may already be stirring in the church. The congregation will grow to understand that it is acceptable to talk about addiction, to bring the "family secret" into the open, and to share the task of recovery with one another.

It is essential to return again and again to the recovery of the congregation while we focus on the recovery of the minister; they are intertwined in one sense, but must also remain independent of one another. This is a difficult process to describe. One recovering minister insightfully notes, "Parishes and clergy get well in the same way—the same issues emerge in much the same way, and often use the same language."

"Detachment" is the process by which the codependent no longer adapts to the addict and the addict's behavior as part of an effort to change it. When adaptation is carried to extremes, the codependent may count the addict's pills, make constant excuses for drunkenness, and minimize the questions raised by others. In the past this was called "enabling," but the use of that term laid blame on the codependent. In detachment both the minister and the congregation must learn to take care of their own needs, asking for help appropriately and allowing others to learn from their mistakes. Detachment is loving limit-setting, and done by choice. It is a response rather than a reaction, and makes us take responsibility for our own personal behavior rather than the behavior of others.

Practice of healthy interpersonal behavior as well as transparency in program and administrative management goes a long way in healing. The day-to-day, attentive presence of the minister allows for a balance of time off for recovery issues, personal education, and the social events so dear to congregational life. This can be coupled with programs that educate members on the spiritual dimensions of prayer and encourage honest self-evaluation. Opportunities for retreats and preaching that teach as well as preach, perhaps using guest clergy, will provide a different perspective about spiritual life. The congregation must go in a different direction now. There will be increased interest in education and wider denominational life as well as issues of global importance helps it break out of the same isolation that so affected its clergy. Rebelliousness and suspiciousness, which is part of the parish's resistance to involving the denominational governing body in its life, will gradually lessen with transparency and time.

Increasing resilience provides a foundation against future dysfunctional behavior as well as assisting the congregations to heal in the present. Prevention will include a practical, step-by-step effort to regularize and make consistant all key areas of parish life, including worship. The need for and benefits of regular worship can be seen most clearly in the reluctance of congregational members to change the times of services; on some level they know that they need this regularity and predictability in their uncertain lives.

Good communication also adds to the ability of the congregation to heal. A "town forum" on a regular (though not necessarily weekly) basis provides an opportunity to clarify and answer questions that various members have as they live out their spiritual and corporate life together. Misunderstandings and the stress of uncertainty can often be relieved by a simple answer, and those who feel conflicted or disagree can find some insight whether or not they agree with the outcome of the conflict. We have already mentioned the need for regular newsletters, updated websites, hard copies of important meeting minutes, and financial reports; all help to create an environment of clear boundaries, responsibility, and mutual understanding.

In several congregations the recovering minister chose to pub-lish his schedule in the weekly or monthly newsletters. (This choice was not any part of the monitoring that occurred while he was still immersed in his addiction.) The format of these daily schedules was varied. For some, it was a calendar of upcoming appointments and obligations, omitting the unexpected pastoral responsibilities that occur in any congregation and, of course, maintaining con-fidentiality. For others, it was a diary or journal of the preceding month that included both pastoral obligations in a general way along with civic and religious involvements, retreats, continuing education, and similar events. This scheduling has a positive effect quite apart from allaying the parish's anxiety over the minister's pre-vious behavior. Perhaps for the first time, the congregation begins to recognize the breadth and complexity of the minister's obliga-tions and responsibilities.

The congregation's spiritual and moral values are important in getting well again, indicating respect for God's gifts to them. In one congregation, an elderly artist was revered as everyone's favor-ite aunt. During her long tenure in the church, her paintings were used on note cards and served as gifts for many events. The way the congregation treated her talent set a model that invited others to share their individual gifts of music, cooking, and gardening.

Insisting on a return to honesty and integrity, frankness and tolerance also allows new members to find a place in the mem-bership of the church. The norms of membership become clearer or are communicated tactfully so that newcomers understand and accept what is asked of them; the hidden agenda is diminished, if not absent. Newcomers are valued for themselves, not for what they can do or pledge. This, of course, indicates that the standards inherent now in the congregation's life are no longer unrealistic. Its members find satisfaction in giving or tithing their income and doing service work in a congregation that allows them enjoyment in their accomplishments.

Sensitive leadership, lay or clerical, will welcome and come to know these newcomers, assess their gifts and whenever possible, encourage them to develop their skills. This is not the same as meeting the newcomer with a fixed agenda. The assessment may be done in a variety of ways, such as through discernment groups, processes for ministry development, and formal assessment of spiritual gifts. Knowing each individual and what they like to do, as well as their employment history, may show the different directions the newcomer might be interested in pursuing, which they themselves may either not recognize or have abandoned earlier in life. It may also, with careful listening, show what is passé in a task that the individual has outgrown. The congregation then is able to share with these individuals both support and sensitivity to their life's purpose and God's purpose for them.

THE SEARCH PROCESS

Sooner or later the recovering minister will retire, be called to a new congregation, or become involved in legalities that will make his continued tenure impossible. Moreover, some denominational bodies, such as the Methodists, move their clergy on a regular basis. Others have developed a complex search process by committee in conjunction with their denominational polity, as in the Episcopal Church, and still others choose new clergy by a congregational vote. This change in congregational leadership should present further opportunities for congregational healing. Even though the congregation has begun healing, the minister's departure and the necessity of change it brings may often be unexpected or provide a very short lead time, thus encouraging a return to a former level of dysfunction. In addition, they hang on to the belief that their minister was "happy in his position and things were so much better."

At the very least there must be an opportunity for goodbyes, with the congregation sharing with one another the best aspects of their ministry together—those times when God seemed truly present. In the best of departures, well-structured ceremonies and goodbyes take place in both formal and informal settings, where an opportunity is provided for each member to offer his or her reflections verbally or in writing. Passing around a Bible in a manner similar to the American Indian "talking stick" offers safe boundaries for each person to say farewell while holding the Bible, a method that allows the speaker an opportunity to speak uninterrupted. The advantage of this method is the recognition of a common ground of feelings and new information by members of the church—a bonding by which members realize the truth of what they have in common. Those people who recognize codependency for what it is and how it disturbs the growth of Christian life will have an opportunity for truth-telling. They are grieving, and whether the minister was perceived as "good or bad," the pain of their loss is still profound.

In a similar manner, the beginning of a grief process must also accompany the leave-taking of a minister whose behavior has caused pain and trouble for the church's members. Ideally a verbal or written apology in order to make amends will lessen the church's sense of betrayal that accompanies their sense of loss. Accountability, or the recognition of its absense, is the beginning of healing. If the minister is unable to be present, a facilitator may direct the process. Rumors, speculation, and half-truths have no place in this transition. Denominational authorities should be involved; trust must be reestablished wherever and whenever possible.

There will always be some good times to remember, although for a long period they will be overshadowed by the problems that caused the minister's leave-taking. Remembering these benefits might focus on a project started by the minister that has continued—such as an outreach project or new ministry of the youth group—and contributes to the wellbeing of the community.

Particularly if there are legal complications that precipitate a sudden and quick departure, it will be difficult to deal with both the parish's sense of betrayal and the dysfunction of the congregation. Some members will also feel abandoned if they had a close relationship with the minister. There is, of course, always the issue of confidentiality and the assumption of innocence until guilt is proven. Each denomination has its own methods for handling these situations, but the more truthfully the incidents can be related, the better. However, it needs to be recognized that different people will hear and take in information on many different levels. Those familiar with addiction will nod wisely; those with family secrets or whose personal needs require them to maintain denial or blame, will be less likely to accept the current situation. That opposition, great or small, should be examined to determine if the search process and concurrent recovery process is proceeding effectively. Some opposition is normal; members exercise power either by leaving or by staying on to air their criticism and complaints. Their input should be valued and acknowledged, however, even encouraged, simply because it are open and direct communication. Sometimes clarification of the search goals and the next steps are all that is needed; some members may simply not be "process-oriented" people.

The activity of developing a congregational life time-line will bring more recent members into the life of the congregation and may well reveal any secrets that have been in the congregation for years. Allowing church members to add their own stories to the time-line over a period of several months will reveal times that have been cherished by its members on an individual as well as community basis. What they valued about their life together and what caused them concern will focus the questions and statements of the search committee. Occasionally, memories of clergy or leadership dysfunction will surface in the conversation with the longtime congregational members. These memories may surprise both those who coordinate the search process and the relevant governing bodies.

Insights from family systems work indicates that disease appears in common underlying issues from generation to generation. Dysfunction exhibits the same patterns with some common issues that progress in severity from minister to minister. A minister with moderate alcoholism may be followed by one who is also a sex addict, followed by another alcoholic minister. Calling a minister of a different gender or with different personal circumstances does appear to provide an opportunity for change in a dysfunctional organization. (However, the new pastor's dysfunction could also take yet another form, such as hidden marital problems.) Again, the minister's behavior is an indicator of the congregation's dysfunction. A better assessment would be to focus on what worked more effectively in the past, in terms of administration and responsibilities, which can then be transposed to the future. The comment that the "good old days are gone" tends to minimize and dismiss the healthy aspects of congregational life that existed before dysfunction began to dominate.

The more involved the congregation can be with one another in the search process and the more trust that the governing body members can build, the less isolated and cut off individual members will feel. Trust and communication between the governing body and the search committee also models optimal behavior for the congregation. Although most congregations insist that they know everyone and their attitudes, it is unlikely that this is true. Not only are many strangers to one another, except in very small churches, but also the belief that the opinions and preferences of members are all the same is usually inaccurate. The congregation has from time to time experienced periods of growth, and the longtime members will have formed their own small groups based on familiarity and life experience. Newcomers do the same, with only occasional forays into one another's territory. As a result, their infrequent conversation is superficial and social, without building relationships or making an effort to find common ground.

Allowing the congregation to see and hear the opinions of others in a town meeting focused on the betrayal and circumstances surrounding the minister's departure is only the beginning of healing opportunities provided by the search process. Each segment of the search process can be planned to increase opportunities for getting to know each other in a healthy and new manner. Some congregational evaluation as well as search processes allow for one-on-one interviews. Ordinarily this would be an opportunity to share meaningful events in the lives of the congregation. However, when dysfunction is great, members engaged in the interview process are encouraged to take this occasion to clarify conversations or experiences they have had that worry or concern them. Furthermore, members who engage in such conversations must be trained and encouraged not to minimize or deprecate anything they are told regarding the experience of another member. If they are unable to make a response, they would best bring the concerns to the ministry committee so that questions can be answered, truth confronted, and clarity stressed.

In the process of these conversations, the amount of jargon and other kinds of language that falls outside the norms of the denomination will also provide an indicator of the depth of the dysfunction. There will be times when the meaning of key phrases and terminology seem foreign to one or the other of the church members; as we have said earlier we are often insensitive to our own use of jargon. A common language should emerge that improves communication about polity, finances, and congregational or administrative structure. Again, the goal of this part of the process is to find a familiar method of communication in the congregation that reduces isolation and promotes healing.

Using the severity of addiction in the minister as a gauge of the level of dysfunction in the congregation has diagnostic applications. As we have learned from the family systems field, like seeks like. Hence marriage seeks its own level of health, and the same appears to be true of families and communities that are impaired by addiction. Trust and truth, control and loss of control, disturb the balance we described in the image of the life raft at the beginning of our discussion of codependency. The level of dysfunction may also be used to define the kind of ministry and the length of time an interim situation might be necessary as well as to determine the skills needed by the interim rector to promote healing.

If there is an interim minister, he or she needs to be organized, attentive to detail, able to tell the truth, and sensitive to the history of the congregation. A person who can collaborate easily and openly with the local governing body, and is unbiased about the nature of the previous minister's departure, can model appropriate behavior for the congregation. Some denominations offer interim minister training that teaches clergy to use the opportunities offered by the transition to make or update changes in the congregation's life. However, change for change's sake at the whim of an interim minister serves only to increase anxiety and to transform a relatively healthy congregation into one that is immobilized by too much volatility. Evaluation and analysis should precede action, even though most clergy transitions take a year or even eighteen months under the best of circumstances. A dysfunctional congregation may require a longer period of time before the search begins to stabilize their behavior, like letting a broken leg heal before beginning rehabilitation to use the leg again.

Obviously the goal of the search process is to find a new minister with the right kind of professional skills and personal gifts required for these congregations to make a healthy recovery. Each step along the way should be examined as to its secondary value of returning the congregation to health. Does the method in use help facilitate member communication, reduce isolation, introduce aspects of reality into congregational myths, and help with truth-telling about the congregation or the former minister? All of these issues need change that is supported by written or educational information, spiritual foundations, and liturgical worship, including prayer. This means that a new mission statement—if that is a denominational norm—or a common understanding of mission if it is not, provides a foundation for any step forward. Each congregation has a unique identity inherent in its founding, in its struggles, and in the context of its community. What is unique about this congregation? What behavior, interests, and goals persist despite the normal changes of growth or decline? If there is stalling or reluctance at examining and reformulating the mission statement, why is it being "sent to committee"? Honest timelines of congregational life accompanied by thoughtful reflection would yield fruitful information on the congregation's core values, their vocation and future direction in their current environment and context. For example, the positive memory of women's groups that comes up in a congregational assessment can be transformed into an outreach project of a woman's group that assists victims of domestic violence.

Then, looking at the history of clergy who have been called over time to this congregation, are there the same common personality traits in the ministers year after year? Take, for example, a congregation whose minister died suddenly right before Christmas, leaving a wife and three small children; followed by another minister who committed suicide six months after he resigned, leaving a wife and school-aged children; followed by an alcoholic minister, also with small children; and eventually followed by still another who was always short of money and needed a driver in order to make congregational visits. The pattern of physical and mental illness is reinforced with each succeeding call to ministry in the congregation.

A more overt issue in times of clergy transition is the issue of power and control. The departure of the minister leaves a vacuum that may be quickly filled by older and wiser leaders, but also by those who for some time have wanted a power position in the congregation. New leadership may initially be valued, but if these members are relatively newcomers to the congregation, the desire for attraction of power that is hidden behind the Christian values of service they espouse will quickly emerge. That is one reason why detailed job descriptions, along with the recognition of clear boundaries and job sharing, will promote a healthier environment for the future healing of the congregation.

We have already mentioned congregations that have changed ministers because they felt that the minister was "a poor fit." However the minister came to be called or placed in the congregation, it is something like a "blind date" in which the couple meet at the whim of friends, or perhaps on the basis of reputation, and never reveal their true selves. The same can hold true for a search process. The qualities that attract the congregation to the minister can be superficial or subliminal at best. One congregation, for example, hired a minister who was bald, a characteristic he shared with a much-loved former minister. The latter's long tenure had been followed by a short stay, which seemed to require them to return to the safety of "the good old days." Over the years we have discovered a return to the "old days" occurs frequently with a focus upon the most beloved qualities of a former minister. The search committee conveniently found other attractive characteristics and common behaviors that helped them place one balding candidate at the top of their list.

The search process that works best examines core values that are essentially part of the congregation's norms. In a dysfunctional congregation, those norms may have eroded over time. As a result, the members must look for them in their history and in their current interactions. What did they most value about their favorite minister? What do they remember with great fondness about some personal aspect of their life in the congregation? What concerns them the most about their life over the years as a congregation, and what exactly seems to be missing? Taking the time to discover all of the major facets of the congregation's life together and then coming to know the clergy who apply for the position or who are placed in the position, will take the "blind" aspect out of the mutual arrangement for a ministry together and for the shared mission in their renewed life in Christ. Reflection and insight, affirmation and encouragement, sharing the journey with one another into a new place where health and holiness are goals and purposes that a recovering congregation can embrace as part of the resurrection experience in their life together.

We all celebrate the end of a search process that brings a new minister into a healing or healthy congregation with all the hope and expectation that life in Christ offers to them. The search process can be a transition time, a time for renewal, reflection, and recovery of the spirit that inspired them to form a Christian community initially. The healthy congregation provides resources to its members to both grow into the fullness of Christ and work together to carry forward God's mission to the world. Congregations have told us when they have moved well into health that the hard times, in retrospect, were occasions of grace, when the power of God to heal and renew was revealed in full measure

> Through many dangers, toils and snares,
> I have already come;
> 'Tis grace hath brought me safe thus far,
> And grace will lead me home.
>
> —From John Newton, "Amazing Grace"

APPENDIX I

*Twelve Steps for Clergy Recovering
from Codependency*

1. Admitted we were powerless over our congregations and that our codependent behavior was making our lives unmanageable.

2. Came to believe that, while we did not have the solution, God in Jesus through the power of the Spirit is the solution to our dilemma.

3. Made the decision to turn our lives and our ministries over to the care of God as we know God in the Crucified and Risen One, seeking to trust fully.

4. Made a searching and fearless moral inventory of ourselves, never shrinking from the examination of our behavior in all matters involving the congregation.

5. Took the risk of telling ourselves, God, and one other carefully chosen person the exact nature of our participation in the situations we face.

6. Became willing to allow God to change us and show us new ways to serve in our ministries.

7. Humbly asked God to make us a new people, to show us new ways of thinking and believing, removing those defects that we uncovered in our moral inventory.

8. Made a list of those to whom we owe an apology or an honest conversation, and became willing to do our part in restoring those relationships, praying for discernment.

9. Made direct amends to those people, except when to do so would injure them or others, always keeping in mind the demands of confidentiality.

10. Adopted a regular discipline of self-examination and became determined to monitor any codependent behavior.

11. Sought through prayer and meditation, continuing education, reading, and honest conversation to develop our own spirituality, and learned to pray only for God's will uniting ourselves to Jesus in Gethsemane.

12. Promised to be honest with others, to broaden the application of these principles to include all our relationships, and to share our story with other clergy without judging or competing with them, never isolating ourselves from the fellowship of those who are truly committed to spiritual growth in Christ.

APPENDIX II

*Twelve Steps for Recovery of
Addictive Congregations*

1. We admitted we were powerless over our past and our addicted clergy, and that our community life had become unmanageable.
2. We came to believe that God, who inspired us to gather as the body of Christ and from whom we have become separated, seeks to grant us reconciliation and healing.
3. We made a decision to turn our individual and community life over to the care of God in Christ and, through the power and help of the Holy Spirit, receive those gifts.
4. We sought in our past those behaviors that separated us from God and the mission that God calls us to share, and fearlessly examined the ways we had strayed from that journey.
5. We admitted openly to the entire congregation, to God, and to those people who were asked to assist us in recovery those behaviors and faithlessnesses that led us astray.
6. We became entirely ready and willing to allow God to change and transform us, and to show us the gifts that he has given us.
7. We humbly asked God to make us a new people, to show us new ways of thinking and believing, and to remove those behaviors and fears that we uncovered in our self-examination.
8. We made a list of those people whom we had betrayed, and became willing to do our part in restoring these relationships with God's help.

9. We made amends to one another through personal and direct contact whenever possible, except when to do so would violate confidentiality and charity.

10. We practiced a regular yearly ministry review of our congregation and clergy, paying particular attention to any codependent behavior patterns.

11. We sought through prayer and meditation, education, and reflection to develop insight and grow into the will of God for our life together, and, with God's help, pray for his guidance in all our congregation's decisions.

12. We promised to share our holiness and growth in grace and to continue to practice these principles in our administration, our corporate life, and our worship in order to deepen, enrich, and strengthen our relationship with God in Christ.

APPENDIX III

*Sample Policy for Alcohol Use
in Congregations*

ST. PAUL'S EPISCOPAL CHURCH
27 Pleasant Street, Brunswick, Me. 04101
207-725-5342
stpauls@stpaulsmaine.org

GUIDELINES FOR ALCOHOL USE

We believe that alcohol consumption is a personal decision, but, if consumed, should be done responsibly. At the same time, we recognize that a significant number of persons who attend or visit our church struggle with addiction. We also strive to respect the many people who come to St. Paul's for AA or other 12-step groups. Therefore, we do not encourage the use of alcohol, but on occasions in which it is used at functions, our aim is to illustrate that it is possible for responsible alcohol use and abstinence to co-exist. When Jesus turned water into wine at the wedding at Cana in John 2:1–11, he did this to reveal his glory to the disciples, not to encourage alcohol use. Church group functions endeavor to reflect the glory and love of God. The spirit underlying these guidelines, therefore, is one that seeks to focus on gathering people together in fellowship. We hope that groups outside of St. Paul's share in this spirit of hospitality.

This policy should not be understood as an encouragement for alcohol use at church functions, and St. Paul's groups that are considering a function with alcohol use should carefully consider the pros and cons of having alcohol at the event.

These guidelines apply to all activities sponsored by St. Paul's Church or by one of its groups, whether the sponsored activity is held at St. Paul's Church or off of St. Paul's property. These guidelines also apply to all non-church groups that use our church space for their own events, receptions, civic group meetings, concerts, etc. Please adhere to these guidelines:

PROMOTION

1. The offering of alcohol may not be advertised or promoted in St. Paul's communications, and will not be the primary purpose of the event.
2. No alcohol may be served at a function which is sponsored in whole or in part by a Youth Group.
3. Alcohol may not be served or consumed at an activity on the grounds of St. Paul's, or at a formal church activity held off the grounds of St. Paul's, unless its use has been formally approved in advance by the St. Paul's Vestry.
4. Should a St. Paul's group or organization desire to serve or use alcohol at one of its activities, that group or organization must formally approve such use, and then forward a request to the Vestry for final approval.
5. Because St. Paul's opens its doors to 12-Step groups, we ask that you take responsibility in learning if any groups are meeting during your own event. If so, please notify that group well in advance that you will be serving alcohol at your event. You may contact the Parish Office for such information.

PURCHASING, SERVING, AND STORING

1. Only beer and still and sparkling wines may be served on St. Paul's property or at St. Paul's events.
2. At those events where a permit is required, alcohol should be served from a single location. (See below for more information about permits).

3. The group responsible for the event must ensure that a responsible adult is overseeing the alcohol at all times, and is maintaining appropriate control over serving it to guests.

4. Youth (21 and under) are prohibited from serving alcohol. All applicable federal, state, and local laws and ordinances, including those governing the serving of alcoholic beverages to those under 21, must be observed. Those under 21 may, however, may be present at functions where wine is served.

5. Alcohol should always be served with food. Be sure to label any food that contains alcohol.

6. Non-alcoholic alternatives must be offered and be equally available and accessible. These alternatives should be served with equal dignity and hospitality and available in the same drinking containers as alcohol, such as in wine glasses.

7. It is the responsibility of the group in charge of the activity to ensure that responsible adults are monitoring use to determine if any persons have become intoxicated, to ensure that any such persons have no further access to alcohol, and to ensure that the person has a safe means for traveling home.

8. All opened bottles must be removed immediately from the premises at the conclusion of the function and unopened bottles must be properly stored and locked or removed from church property.

APPLICATIONS

1. Any St. Paul's group seeking to provide alcohol at an activity on or off the grounds of St. Paul's, or any group from outside of St. Paul's seeking to provide alcohol at an activity at St. Paul's Church or on its grounds, must submit to the St. Paul's office a completed "Application for Alcohol Use" form. This form should be submitted sufficiently in advance of the event to provide the Vestry time to consider and act on the application. Please recall that no alcohol can be served on St. Paul's grounds or at a St. Paul's sponsored event without prior approval by the St. Paul's Vestry. The Vestry will not approve any application that does not include with it a State of Maine "Application for License for Incorporated Civic Organization" that has already been approved by appropriate state or local officials.

2. Any non-church group or individual that is requesting approval to serve alcohol at an event being held on the grounds of St. Paul's

Church, in addition to complying with other requirements in this policy, must submit documentation of host liquor liability insurance coverage for the event, including documentation that St. Paul's is named as an additional insured on the policy.

3. The Vestry has complete discretion to approve or reject any "Application for Alcohol Use" relating to any St. Paul's event or to any event on St. Paul's grounds.

4. It is vitally important to note that if a St. Paul's group or a group outside of St. Paul's charges admission for an event at which alcohol is served (even if they are not selling the alcohol), they must obtain a temporary liquor permit from the State of Maine.

STATE PERMITS

State temporary alcohol permits must be filed for functions serving wine and charging an admission fee, and are limited to five (5) per year per group that uses St. Paul's. St. Paul's groups are also included in this limit. The permit must be signed by the Cumberland County Clerk's office and approved by the State of Maine Department of Public Safety in a timely manner. While the application for this permit is attached, you can obtain an original copy at the following address:

The State of Maine
Liquor Licensing & Inspection Division
164 State House Station
Augusta ME 04333-0164
Tel: (207) 624-7220 Fax: (207) 287-3424
http://www.maine.gov/dps/liqr/index.html

Thank you for your willingness to comply with these guidelines.

ST. PAUL'S EPISCOPAL CHURCH
27 Pleasant Street, Brunswick, ME 04011
207-725-5342

SUGGESTED READING

Stephen P. Apthorp, *Alcohol and Substance Abuse: A Handbook for Clergy and Congregations* (Lincoln, NE: iUniverse, 2003).

Cash, Margie, "Codependency in the Church" (*Margiecash.com* 2007).

Carlos C. Clemente, *Addiction and Change: How Addiction Develops and Addicted People Recover* (New York: Guilford Press, 2006).

Edwin H. Friedman, *Generation to Generation* (New York: Guilford Press, 1985).

Edwin H Freidman, *A Failure of Nerve* (New York: Church Publishing, 2007).

Gerald May, *Addiction and Grace* (San Francisco: Harper, 1992).

Craig Nakken, *Reclaim Your Family from Addiction* (Center City, MN: Hazelden, 2000).

Denis G. Meacham *The Addiction Ministry Handbook: A Guide for Congregations* (Boston: Skinner House, 2004).

Platt, Nancy, "Betrayal and Healing: The Aftermath of the Judas Kiss," *Journal of Pastoral Care and Counseling* 59:4 (2005).

Recovery Ministries of the Episcopal Church:

Linda A. Meyer, "Intervention"

Linda A. Meyer, "Enabling"

Janee Parnegg, "The Functional Alcoholic"

Samuel Shoemaker, "What the Church Can Learn from AA"

Peter L. Steinke, *Healthy Congregations: A Systems Approach* (Herndon, VA: Alban, 2006).

Peter L. Steinke, *Congregational Leadership in Anxious Times* (Herndon, VA: Alban, 2006).

Doug Thorburn, *How to Spot Hidden Alcoholics* (Northridge, CA: Galt, 2004).

Abraham J. Twerski, *Addictive Thinking: Understanding Self Deception* (Center City, MN: Hazelden, 1997).